I0092885

THE RADIANT TEEN

BOOST YOUR CONFIDENCE, CREATE LASTING FRIENDSHIPS, AND THRIVE IN SOCIAL SITUATIONS

MARNIE DAVID

Copyright © 2024 by Marnie David
All rights reserved.
No part of this book may be reproduced in any form or by any electronic or
mechanical means, including information storage and retrieval systems, without
written permission from the author, except for the use of brief quotations in a book
review.

CONTENTS

THE CONFIDENT TEEN

THE SOCIAL TEEN

THE CONFIDENT TEEN

A PRACTICAL GUIDE TO BOOST YOUR CONFIDENCE, TRANSFORM YOUR SELF-WORTH, AND TAKE CONTROL OF YOUR LIFE

Copyright © 2023 by Marnie David. All rights reserved.

No part of this book may be reproduced in any form or by any electronic or mechanical means, including information storage and retrieval systems, without written permission from the author, except for the use of brief quotations in a book review.

Disclaimer

Although the publisher and the author have made every effort to ensure that the information in this book was correct at press time and while this publication is designed to provide accurate information in regard to the subject matter covered, the publisher and the author assume no responsibility for errors, inaccuracies, omissions, or any other inconsistencies herein and hereby disclaim any liability to any party for any loss, damage, or disruption caused by errors or omissions, whether such errors or omissions result from negligence, accident, or any other cause.

The publisher and the author make no guarantees concerning the level of success you may experience by following the advice and strategies contained in this book, and you accept the risk that results will differ for each individual. The testimonials and examples provided in this book show exceptional results, which may not apply to the average reader, and are not intended to represent or guarantee that you will achieve the same or similar results.

FREE SELF REFLECTION JOURNAL!
The 10 Best Journal Prompts to Unlock Your Authentic Self!

THE **CONFIDENT TEEN**

Download my journal freebie to get a head start on
understanding and accepting yourself for who you are.

INTRODUCTION

Picture this: it's a bright summer's day, and everywhere you look, the world seems to shine with endless possibilities.

The air is filled with the sound of laughter and carefree joy, especially from a group of giggling ten-year-olds nearby. Their energy and giddiness are tangible. Yet, amid the backdrop of your bustling thoughts, you can't help but find them . . . annoying.

Wait a minute, you think, feeling a jolt of alarm and introspection. *Wasn't that me not too long ago? Why didn't I notice how exasperating I was? But it's just innocent laughter . . . Why am I so bothered by this, anyway?!*

Then it hits you: you're standing at a one-way threshold. Sweet independence is calling, and the weight of expectation is growing a little heavier every day. As the sun's rays warm your skin, a burning question fills every cell in your body.

When does a kid become an adult?

I remember contemplating that same question when I was a teen. It was especially bad one afternoon when I was so upset, I just had to get away from everyone and everything. After a long walk, I plopped onto a bench in the park.

"Long day?"

The voice came from the other side of the bench and belonged to a man with years and years etched into his face. He had the gentlest eyes and a smile that seemed to hold all the answers.

"You know," he said as if he could hear the questions running rampant in my mind, "when I was a kid, I had heard the words 'Now you're a real man' so many times. My first hunting trip, the day I got my driver's license . . . The time I told my brother I had kissed a girl for the first time!"

We shared a chuckle.

"But as I got older, the issue weighed heavier and heavier on me. Then, on my fifteenth birthday, I finally mustered up the courage to ask my mom when I would *officially* be an adult. And you'll never believe it, but . . ."

I leaned forward, eager to soak in his wisdom.

"This morning I woke up and I just can't seem to remember the exact moment I became an adult!"

I frowned, pursing my lips as I tried to ignore his infectious laughter this time.

"But don't worry," he continued, his eyes full of reassurance, "you're already on the train, and it's going to be an interesting ride from here on out. There will be unimaginable experiences, there will be bumps, and there will be important stops along the way—but none of them will be *the moment*."

"I don't get it," I grumbled.

The man leaned back on the bench, his gaze drifting to the distant horizon of nostalgia. "Adulthood isn't marked by some grand milestone. It's a journey of learning from your mistakes, embracing responsibility, and cultivating the qualities that will turn you into the person you want to be."

He turned to me. "Want to know the secret to it all?"

I nodded.

"I'll tell you. But only if you promise to pass it on one day."

"I promise."

He smiled. "Confidence."

"That's it?"

"Sure! It's the armor that shields you from doubt, the fuel that propels you forward . . . no matter what, and the light that guides your path."

To be honest, it sounded easy—totally within my reach, you know? What the man didn't tell me, what I had to discover for myself is that like anything worthwhile in life, it takes deliberate practice to build confidence. No matter where you come from, what school you attend, what classes you take, what extracurricular activities you do, who you hang out with, or how popular you are, no one is born confident. Don't let anyone convince you otherwise, ever.

The transition from childhood to adulthood is exciting, but it's also littered with difficulties. And where you are right now, at this crossroads called adolescence, is especially challenging. In between getting to know yourself and developing your own values, beliefs, and interests, you have intense stuff to deal with . . .

- Dealing with your friends, making new ones, fitting in, and navigating all that social pressure.
- Getting good grades, taking extra classes, preparing for college entrance exams, and not to mention the extracurriculars.
- Being a good family member, even if you find those people annoying sometimes!

- Learning to accept and love yourself.

These things can cause some serious stress and make you unsure of yourself, which sucks because it only doubles the pressure. Yeah, I know *exactly* how you feel.

But you know what? It's OK. You're OK. Everything you're feeling and thinking is normal.

Think of your teenage years as life's boot camp. It's a rite of passage. And once you get to the other side, you'll have the skills to take on anything life can throw at you.

But all of us, no matter how old we are, need a little help.

I say this knowing that my teenage self is rolling her eyes at me. Because growing up, I wasn't exactly a fan of asking for help.

Despite learning the secret to taking control of my life from that kind man in the park, I didn't know how to implement it. My twin sister, Casey, had the whole confidence thing down, which just made things worse for me. While we were in school, I never asked her how she did it, because then I'd have to admit that I was scared and couldn't figure stuff out on my own. And so I pretended I was fine. I did many things to please my friends (and sometimes even my family) just to feel included. Whatever I did, I never let my guard down. But at night, alone in my bed, where no one could see me, I felt so alone and lost.

It took me ages to become a confident person. Now, I'd be lying if I said my teenage years were all bad, but I know for sure it would've been easier if I had the right tools and guidance (and the guts to ask for help).

When I became a teacher, I developed an intense desire to instill confidence in my students. I knew they'd have a massive advantage in life if they could face challenges with the confidence I never had as a teen. While brainstorming how I could teach them to be confident, I remembered my sister. So, after all those years, I finally asked Casey how she had managed to be so confident when we were growing up.

"Me? Confident?" She blushed. "Guess I faked it pretty well!"

Ha! I wasn't alone, after all.

But I didn't want my students to fake it. And, having welcomed my first son into the world, I certainly didn't want him to fake it. They all deserved better, and I wanted them to use that secret ingredient to their full advantage. So, I started coming up with creative ways to teach my students everything I had learned about the art of building confidence. Day by day, I saw the positive impact it had on them. You, too, deserve to live with confidence and an unshakable sense of self-worth. Your teenage years should be some of the *best* years of your life—not the easiest, but definitely among the best.

(Spoiler: Life doesn't get easier when you grow up. You just learn to deal with it like a pro. And confidence helps. Like, a lot!)

Whatever your personal circumstances, and whatever is holding you back, you should know you *can* overcome it. Seriously—I've worked with young people from all walks of life, and if there's one thing I've learned, it's that if you really want things to change, nothing in the world can stop you from making it happen.

You've already taken the first step toward more confidence and becoming a stronger, better you by reading this far. All you have to do to unlock your full potential is read on.

See you in Chapter One!

CHAPTER 1
UNDERSTANDING CONFIDENCE

> *"Confidence isn't walking into a room thinking you're better than everyone. It's walking in and not having to compare yourself to anyone at all."*

DWAYNE ('THE ROCK') JOHNSON

Sure sounds easy . . . Until you're in a room comparing yourself to your classmates, right?

After talking with that nice man in the park, I felt super sure of myself. And why wouldn't I? I had the secret to overcoming all the obstacles on my journey to adulthood: confidence, my new superpower.

But when I got home, uncertainty hit me like a roller-coaster drop. In just one afternoon, I was back to feeling insecure, and my self-doubt had grown even stronger by bedtime.

The struggle is real . . .

If self-doubt takes you on roller coaster rides, don't feel ashamed —it's totally normal. The good news is that you're not at the mercy of those roller coaster rides. With guidance, you can take control and become confident despite the doubt.

In this chapter, we'll unravel the mysteries surrounding confidence and debunk myths that might be holding you back. You'll gain the knowledge to navigate adolescence with self-assurance and learn to embrace and own your unique strengths, quirks, and imperfections with pride.

WHAT IS CONFIDENCE?

Have you ever studied really hard for a test and just *knew* you'd ace it? Or trained like crazy for a sports event or a competition and *knew* you had it in you to win?

That's confidence.

When you're confident, you feel sure of yourself and believe in your abilities, even in the face of tough challenges. You also take pride in your individuality and your actions show that you embrace your quirks. But it's not about acting superior. It's about saying, "I can do this," and genuinely believing it in your heart. It doesn't stop there, though. Confidence also involves acting on that belief in yourself.

The most important thing to remember about confidence is that it's a skill you can improve with practice by building a confident mindset, comparing yourself kindly (because we all have our unique talents!), and overcoming self-doubt.

Does being confident mean you'll never doubt yourself again?

Nope. Self-doubt will always find a way to creep in. Even the most confident people experience fear and uncertainty. Confidence just means pushing through and not allowing self-doubt to stop you from living life and being the best version of yourself.

RECAP: AN EASY EQUATION FOR DEFINING CONFIDENCE

• • •

Confidence = (Believe in your abilities + Embrace your individuality) + (Act on your belief in yourself) + (Push through, no matter what + Practice a confident mindset)

In short: $C = (B+E) + (A) + (P+P)$

Now, remember: Confidence means BEAPP up!

In other words: Confidence means believing in your abilities and embracing your individuality. When you're confident, you act on your beliefs, push through when things get tough, and practice a confident mindset every day.

WHAT CONFIDENCE IS NOT

Emily, an energetic 16-year-old, never had a shy bone in her body. Having a competitive spirit and being academically strong, she believed she could become a valuable member of the school's debate team. The team was impressed with how much she knew and welcomed her with enthusiasm. During the first debate, Emily dominated the conversation, often overpowering her opponents with her loud voice and strong opinions. The opposing team soon lost interest in the debate. And by the time it was all over, Emily's own team seemed distant and unimpressed with her clear win for them. Then the team leader approached her and said, "This isn't going to work out."

Confidence is not arrogance

Emily's story is a brilliant example of the fine line that exists between being confident and having an arrogance about you. Remember, confidence is a belief in yourself and what you can achieve. It's not a belief that you're better than others. True confidence is about being secure in yourself without diminishing the worth of your classmates or the people you meet. True confidence is lifting others up and recognizing their strengths, too.

Note: Being bold doesn't necessarily make you arrogant. The defining factor lies in how and why you use it, and especially in how you treat other people while using boldness to your advantage.

Confidence is not perfection

Don't waste your energy trying to be flawless or thinking everyone expects you to have all the answers when you're confident. True confidence is being able to smile and say, "I don't have the answer, but I'll try my best to find it!" It's about embracing your imperfections and believing in yourself despite doubts and mistakes.

Confidence isn't dependent on external factors

It's easy to assume that confidence comes from things like appearance, popularity, or achievements—but it doesn't. While external validation like receiving praise when helping others or getting good grades are useful indicators that you're on the right track, they don't define you as a confident person. The source of confidence lies inside you, regardless of everything happening on the outside.

Confidence is not the absence of fear

Even the most confident people have fears, but they take action despite them. That's because confidence is having the courage to step outside of your comfort zone and pursue your goals, even when it feels scary.

"I used to be so afraid of public speaking that I would throw up before I went on stage. I would get so nervous that I would shake, and my voice would quiver. But I learned how to overcome my anxiety and now I love public speaking. I actually get energized by it."

TONY ROBBINS

Confidence is unique

There's no blueprint for what a confident person looks like, or how they talk or act. Some people may be more outgoing and bolder, while others may be reserved and introspective, but they can be equally confident. Confidence is, after all, about being true to yourself and embracing your unique strengths and qualities.

RECAP: CONFIDENCE IS NOT . . .

Confidence is not arrogance, perfection, or a life without fear. It doesn't depend on outside factors but on what's inside of you. Finally, confidence looks different for everyone because we're all unique.

WHY DOES CONFIDENCE MATTER?

Confidence is the foundation you need to build a fulfilling life. It opens doors, propels you forward, and empowers you to live without limits. Let's explore specific areas of life where it pays to be confident.

Confidence helps you overcome fear and anxiety

How many times have you really, *really* wanted to do something but came up with a rock-solid excuse not to and regretted it afterward? Or how many times have you looked the other way to keep the peace despite seeing something wrong happening?

The above examples are classic results of fear and anxiety. Pretty annoying, right? This may come as a surprise, but fear and anxiety are actually good for you because they protect you in genuinely dangerous situations.

So, your mission is not to banish fear and anxiety altogether, but to understand when it's helpful and when it's just holding you back from living. Confidence is a powerful ally in helping you spot the difference, and it gives you the strength to overcome challenges and grow beyond your comfort zone.

Confidence makes you resilient in the face of challenges

It's one thing to overcome the fear of facing life's challenges, but after conquering the fear, what do you do when things go wrong?

Like, what do you do when your crush crushes your spirit by saying no after you ask them on a date? Or what do you do when the class bully snickers to mock you and influences your classmates to look at you funny when you're about to do a presentation?

A powerful byproduct of confidence is the ability to bounce back, shrug your shoulders, and march on with pride—better known as resilience. Sure, it's going to hurt if someone breaks your heart or tries to embarrass you, and sometimes it'll be difficult to complete tasks and push through challenges. But as a confident teen, you'll have the resilience to make things work—you'll either find a solution or walk away with your self-assurance intact when things don't work out.

Confidence helps you make the best of bad situations

My high school English teacher had a bright yellow classroom, and the walls were full of inspirational and motivational quotes. One of them was in the front of the classroom, right above the blackboard.

> "If you fail to plan, you plan to fail."
>
> BENJAMIN FRANKLIN

Sound advice, but it can also make life harder than it needs to be if you don't add flexibility into the mix. That's because, sometimes, you can make the best and most well-thought-out plans, only to have life throw curveballs and shatter those plans.

> "Life is what happens to you when you're busy making other plans."
>
> JOHN LENNON

Plans don't always work out. And to keep your sanity, you need to be OK with that. Be flexible so you can adapt and find creative solutions. Confidence helps you to stay positive, make the best of the messes you might find yourself in, and turn challenges into opportunities.

Confidence gives you a better outlook on life

Imagine a confident you applying for your dream job or pursuing your passions. Just by believing in yourself and your abilities, you're already setting yourself apart from others and increasing your chances of success.

OK, so maybe you're not in the job market yet, but that's not the point. Confident people ooze all the right stuff to stand out. Whether you want to become the captain of your sports team, lead a school committee, get that part-time job you've been eyeing, or whatever your heart desires, your chance of being noticed and chosen is higher when you're confident.

Confidence helps you make choices that are good for you

Of all the things I had to shake off in life, my need to please people was one of the hardest. I felt like I had this obligation to be a good person, and if I didn't do the things people asked, it meant I was a terrible person and friend. Well, I later learned that saying no doesn't make you a bad person. It makes you confident, respectable, and dependable.

You have the right to make your own choices. So, say no to that party invitation, a day out with your friends, or when someone offers you a cigarette—and do it without shame.

It's almost impossible to trust yourself in the face of decisions when you lack confidence. You'll constantly seek validation from others and do things because *they* think it's a good idea. It's a recipe for personal frustration and disappointment. If you decide to do anything at all, you should do it because it's *your* choice, not because your friends are doing it, not because you're worried that *not* doing it will make you look bad, and not because it's expected of you. When you're confident, you know that every choice you make is your own and that it's good for *you*.

(Disclaimer: I'm not encouraging you to say no when your mom, dad, or guardian asks you to do your chores! That's different.)

Confidence helps you build authentic relationships

When you exude self-assurance, it creates a welcoming aura that makes others feel comfortable around you and opens up channels for clear communication, which can prevent misunderstandings and promote stronger connections.

Confidence also makes you assertive. You can stand up for yourself by drawing boundaries and communicating your needs clearly but respectfully. However, a relationship is a two-way street, so you need to be able to listen, too. Here, too, confidence saves the day, because you'll be less preoccupied with self-doubt and be able to really focus when someone else speaks. This makes you empathetic and a strong ally who your friends can rely on.

RECAP: WHY YOU SHOULD CARE ABOUT BEING CONFIDENT

Because when you're confident, you can CONNECT with your true self and live life to the fullest.

Conquer fears and embrace opportunities.
Overcome challenges with resilience.
Navigate life's twists and turns with positivity.
Never make choices that don't feel right to you.
Elevate your outlook on life.
Communicate effectively for better relationships.
Trust yourself.

THE SCIENCE OF CONFIDENCE

No worries—we're not diving into boring formulas or undecipherable theories here. We'll just chat about some important stuff you need to know.

But . . . Why? Science sucks!

I know.

Yet beyond the classroom, science is fascinating. There are a ton of research topics, and while many of them are pretty meh, others are amazing, like the science of confidence, psychology, and how the brain works. They're super important fields because they help people understand themselves so much better. And, no, you don't need to become an expert to fully appreciate what your mind can do for you. Hopefully, this section will spark your interest in learning more about how your brain works from a psychological and neuroscientific point of view.

Still not impressed? OK, here's why it's in your best interest to learn about the science of confidence:

- **Awareness is a superpower:** Knowing more about how your brain works empowers you to take control of your life with confidence.
- **Break the myth of perfection:** Research shows that everyone struggles with self-doubt. Learning about it encourages you to accept your imperfections.
- **Rewire your brain:** Positive self-talk, stepping out of your comfort zone, and celebrating small successes actually work. Research supports their effectiveness.
- **Appreciate the chemistry of confidence:** A confident brain leads to happiness, motivation, and a positive outlook on life.
- **Adopt a growth mindset:** Understanding your mind's power and its ability to develop and adapt allows you to embrace a growth mindset and boost your confidence.

Without further ado, let's dive into some sciency goodness.

Epistemic confidence vs. social confidence

What is epistemic confidence?

This type of confidence has to do with how sure you feel about what you know. Here's an example:

> **You:** "Did you know the key to academic success is hard work and putting in regular study time?"
> **Me:** "Really? Are you sure?"
> **You:** "Yup. I've read up on it. Regular study habits improve your memory, understanding, and overall success in exams. And I've tested the theory . . . Since I've been at it more consistently, my grades have gone up."

Here's another example:

You: "This game is terrible. The guy who made it didn't
have good programming skills. You really need a decent
understanding to make great games."
Me: "Really? I heard it was easy . . ."
You: "Why don't you program a game, then?"
Me: "Uh . . ."
You: "It's not easy. I've studied the field since forever. Trust
me, without really good programming skills, there's no
way you can design top-notch games."

In both examples, you showed high epistemic confidence, or a
solid belief in your knowledge, opinions, and conclusions. High
epistemic confidence results from intense study of topics that you
need to know (to graduate) and topics that interest you. This type
of confidence allows you to feel sure of your knowledge and abilities and gives you trust in your own judgment.

However, a pitfall of epistemic confidence is developing a fixed
mindset. Being too certain of your opinions can hinder personal
growth. It's important to keep an open mind and be willing to
adapt when necessary.

What is social confidence?

This is the one we all struggle with sometimes. Social confidence
is about how sure you feel about yourself when dealing with other
people. Let's see it in action:

You: "Hey! Wanna hang out with some of my friends
and me?"
Me: "Mm . . . I'm actually an introvert, so . . ."
You: "Perfect! It's not going to be a crowd or anything like
that. We'll just chill."
Me: "Oh, good! Let's do it, then."

And here's another example:

> **You:** "Hey! Wanna hang out with some of my friends and me?"
> **Me:** "Yes! I love meeting new people."

Would you be surprised if I told you that my character showed confidence in both examples? Parties are one of many social situations you'll find yourself in throughout life. But I used it as an example to make an important point: Being an introvert doesn't make you insecure. You *can* not like crowds and still be the person who oozes self-assurance. So, in the first example, my character only hesitated because she didn't like the idea of having to deal with lots of people, but the moment she realized it would be a small get-together, she was happy to go. (It's not that she couldn't handle a big crowd if she had to, she just has her preferences, and that's OK—we're all unique.)

So, social confidence helps you to relax in social settings and generally makes you more approachable and likable. Moreover, it helps you to listen to others, voice your own opinions, and build authentic relationships.

So, what's the difference, and is one more important than the other?

	EPISTEMIC CONFIDENCE	SOCIAL CONFIDENCE
What is it?	A strong belief in your knowledge, abilities, and opinions.	The ability to feel comfortable and be self-assured when you're interacting with other people.
Focus	Internal: It's about your personal certainty in what you know and that your ideas are worth exploring.	External: It's about building connections and being seen as a confident person by others.
Flexibility	Epistemic confidence can hinder your growth if it makes you resistant to others' opinions or new information that challenges your beliefs.	The antidote to too much epistemic confidence! Social confidence makes you willing to listen, be open to new ideas and experiences, and be adaptable.
Advantages	-Boosts your self-assurance. -Fights self-doubt. -Allows you to take action. -Gives you the boldness to stand up for yourself and defend your beliefs.	-Boosts your social skills. -Helps you build meaningful relationships and friendships. -Promotes a positive self-image.
Example	"I know my stuff!"	"Let me show you how and why I know my stuff, and then you can tell me about the stuff you know."
Is one more important or better than the other?	Nope. Epistemic and social confidence are soulmates. If one suffers, so does the other. Likewise, you can't thrive in one type of confidence without it affecting the other. The more you believe in yourself and what you know, the bigger urge you'll have to stand up for it. And the more comfortable you feel around other people and their opinions, the more you'll want to share what you know and believe.	

Neuroscience and confidence

While psychology helps us understand our behavior better, neuroscience (the study of the brain and nervous system) helps us understand the link between our behaviors and brains.

Can neuroscience help boost confidence?

You bet it can! Thanks to neuroscience, the myth that confidence is bestowed upon a select few at birth has been thoroughly debunked. While some people may be more predisposed to confidence, anyone can develop it. Let's look at how you can use neuroscience to boost your confidence:

Take control of how you respond when things go south

When faced with adversity, your brain releases stress hormones that can lower your confidence. However, when good things happen, your brain releases feel-good hormones that boost confidence. While you can't control every situation, you can control how you respond. By behaving in a way that promotes the release of feel-good hormones, you can prevent your confidence from plummeting.

I used to cringe at the thought of having to speak in front of people. Seriously, just thinking about it triggered nausea and made my palms clammy. Then I learned that hormones could influence confidence, so I decided to put it to the test.

My first mission was learning to speak confidently in front of just five people. With my goal set, the next challenge was to trick my brain into producing more feel-good hormones than stress hormones while I talked in front of people.

My solution? Stand-up comedy.

The first time I stood in front of the mirror to practice, I felt incredibly stupid. But I smiled, straightened my back, and told myself, "You're gonna ace this!"

Before I knew it, my best friend couldn't stop laughing at my jokes. I was dumbstruck but totally satisfied. One day, without even thinking about it, I was telling a joke to *seven* people.

Speaking in front of people still gets me nervous sometimes, but I never back away anymore; I don't get nauseous, and the icky palms are a thing of the past. And if my nerves get me worked up too much, I simply tell a joke to break the ice and get my feel-good hormones flowing.

25

Realize that your brain doesn't always get it right and remind it of your strengths and accomplishments.

Ever made a mistake that made you want to disappear? And then realized it wasn't that bad afterward? What's up with that?

Well, the human brain has a nasty habit. It does this annoying thing where it zooms in on moments of failure, embarrassment, and your weaknesses more than focusing on your strengths and triumphs. So, if you make a mistake, your brain kind of glitches and tells you that you're not good enough. The only reason you may believe this negative self-talk is that you have never questioned those thoughts. But by challenging negativity when it pops up, you can begin to change the way you respond and feel when slip-ups happen.

Build confidence by creating new beliefs about yourself

If you push yourself to participate in activities that require confidence, doubt yourself less, and start feeling comfortable around people, you can effectively change your self-image and what you believe about yourself.

If you currently believe you're not one for group activities, you'll experience stress at first. That's normal. But do your best to avoid coming up with "I can't do this" excuses. I promise, the first one will be the hardest. After that, you'll feel so much better and realize you're stronger than you thought.

Catch confidence from other people . . . Kind of like a cold, but with benefits!

Your brain and nervous system produce mirror neurons that fire up whenever you perform actions or watch others perform actions. This means that your brain can simulate what the other person is doing without you physically doing it yourself.

What does that mean?

Spending time with confident people allows their confidence to rub off on you because your mirror neurons internalize their words and behavior. It's like a contagious effect that influences you to think, talk, and behave more confidently. The best part is that you can catch the confidence bug whether you're physically present with confident people or watching them on a screen. Think about your favorite singer, athlete, or even a cool character from a movie. These role models exude confidence, and as you watch and learn from them, your mirror neurons go wild, allowing you to pick up their confident moves and mindsets.

Fun fact: You can spread confidence, too.

When you believe in yourself and show it to your friends, they can catch your confidence bug. By being self-assured, speaking up, and expressing your opinions, you automatically inspire others to do the same.

Here are some ways to catch and spread the confidence bug:

- Hang out with confident people.
- Emulate positive role models.
- Share and encourage confidence through your own actions.

RECAP: THE SCIENCE OF CONFIDENCE

- It's important to understand the science of confidence because if you know how your brain works, you can take control of your life.
- You get two types of confidence: epistemic and social. Both types are important for your personal growth. You can't have one without the other.
- Neuroscience proves that anyone can acquire and develop confidence.

- You can use your knowledge of neuroscience to boost your confidence. For example, you can use methods like learning to control how you respond to bad situations and changing your relationship with negative beliefs about yourself.
- Confidence is contagious—use it to your advantage!

THE CONFIDENCE-COMPETENCE LOOP

What is it?

Imagine a loop where confidence and competence are intertwined and constantly influencing each other. The cycle starts with the belief in yourself and your abilities (confidence) and propels you to develop the skills and knowledge to back up that belief (competence).

The more confident you are, the more motivated you become to take action and improve your skills. And as you gain competence in a particular area, your confidence grows even more, creating a positive feedback loop.

Think of it this way: Confidence is like the fuel that propels you forward, while competence is the engine that drives your progress.

Why you should care about the confidence-competence loop

A basic understanding of the loop can accelerate your journey of becoming confident in various aspects of your life:

- It will help you overcome fear and anxiety faster.
- It will help you set goals and reach them.
- It can help you enjoy the learning process and stay motivated.

. . .

RECAP: A LOOP FOR LIFE-LONG SUCCESS

Here's an easy way to remember what the confidence-competence loop is and how it works . . . Call it the CCC-Loop:

C > Confidence (believe in yourself and your abilities)

C > Competence (build your skills and knowledge)

C > Circle back! (gain even more confidence and reach your full potential!)

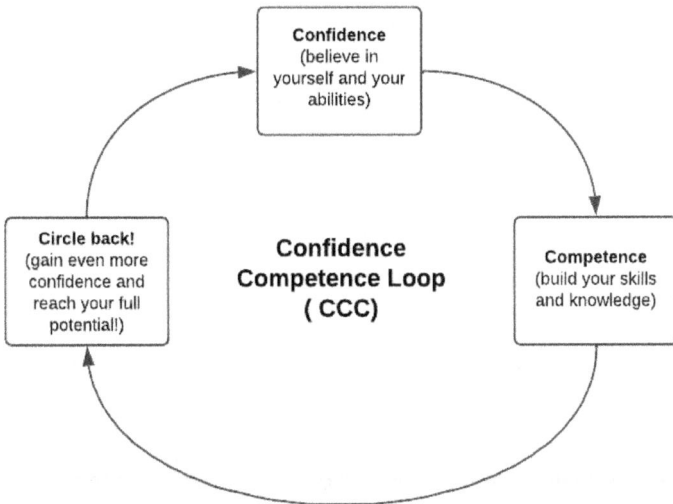

That's a wrap! Now that you know confidence is well within your reach, I bet there's *nothing* that can hold you back from getting it. And you know what? You deserve success, happiness, and an awesome life—so don't settle for anything less.

If you ever need a refresher on anything we talked about in this chapter, head over to the *Recap* part of each section.

In the next chapter, we're going to talk about where self-doubt comes from and, better yet, how you can overcome it. See you on the other side.

END-OF-CHAPTER ACTIVITY: FIND A GROUP ACTIVITY TO BOOST YOUR CONFIDENCE

In a notebook, write down a list of your interests and hobbies. Go through each one and think of ways you can pursue them in a group setting. For example, if your list contains "art," you can write "art workshops" or "art classes" next to it as possible activities. Or, if your list contains "reading," you can add "book club" as a possible activity. If you have "baseball," possible activities could be "ask friends to play for fun" or "try out for the baseball team."

When your list and possible activities are complete, draw a box or circle around your top five choices.

Before you make a final choice, chat about your interests and plans with your friends and family. Don't be shy to ask them what they think about it or even what they think would be a good fit for you. If you can, talk to people who are already doing those activities and ask them any questions that come to mind. It's possible that you'll scratch out one or two activities after your talks.

Take a day or two to think everything over. Imagine yourself participating confidently in each of the remaining activities on your list. Finally, choose the one that resonates with you most, take a deep breath, tell yourself you've got what it takes to do it well, and dive in!

CHAPTER 2
THE ROOTS OF SELF-DOUBT (EXPLORING SELF-DOUBT PART 1)

> "I have self-doubt. I have insecurity. I have fear of failure.
> I have nights when I show up at the arena and I'm like
> 'My back hurts, my feet hurt, my knees hurt. I don't have
> it. I just want to chill.' We all have self-doubt. You don't
> deny it, but you also don't capitulate to it. You embrace
> it."
>
> KOBE BRYANT

You have a friend, Aubrey, who's brilliant, full of positivity, and a bundle of energy whenever you guys are together. He always shares his ideas and dreams with you, but among other people, it's like Aubrey becomes a different person. He becomes quiet and hovers in the background while everyone else does the talking. It's weird because whenever someone mentions a topic you *know* Aubrey is passionate about, it's like he doesn't even care. And it doesn't happen among friends and classmates only—he has told you so many times that he wants to go traveling after he graduates and get away from the family business. But you've never heard him protest when his dad talks about the law schools he should aim to get into.

Now, I know you wouldn't be caught dead admitting it (and neither would your friends if they were reading this!), but I'm pretty sure you get how Aubrey feels. He has self-doubt, and it's making him question himself . . .

- *Am I good enough to voice my opinion?*
- *Does anyone even care about the things I care about?*
- *What if I make a fool of myself?*
- *I'm not even sure I want to study right after high school, but what if I disappoint my parents if I don't?*

At other times, the self-doubt gets a little mean . . .

- *You can't do it. Period.*
- *Not gonna happen . . . You're too much of a wimp.*
- *Don't even think about it! That kid is way better at this than you are.*

Self-doubt happens to all of us, and it doesn't matter how old you get, it's going to accompany you for the rest of your life.

OK. I know that sounds bleak but hear me out.

Self-doubt has its place. It draws the important line between arrogance and confidence. And, coupled with healthy doses of stress, self-doubt serves as a reminder that you are, in fact, just human.

In this chapter, we'll explore what self-doubt is, where it comes from, how it influences you, and how you can tell it to move over so you can be the one at the steering wheel of this thing called life.

WHAT IS SELF-DOUBT?

Self-doubt is that annoying, nagging, second-guessing gremlin sitting on your shoulder. It makes you question your abilities, potential, and worth. It's also the source of negative self-talk, which we'll explore in Chapter 6. Self-doubt can cause insecurity, which is the exact opposite of confidence. If you give in to self-doubt, you might end up thinking you're not as smart, talented, or capable as everyone else.

But here's the truth: Self-doubt is just a feeling. It doesn't define who you are or determine your potential.

Besides, how much power does a pesky little gremlin have if you can just flick it off your shoulder when it misbehaves? Granted, you can never get rid of it, but every time you flick it off, you'll send a clear message that *you're* in control. Eventually, that little gremlin will learn to behave (as best it can) and become quieter.

Self-doubt is normal and OK, as long as you don't allow it to stop you from growing, expanding your boundaries, and living life to the fullest.

And let's face it, arrogance is just a defense mechanism against feelings of intense insecurity. So, if you have to deal with an arrogant classmate, don't take them seriously. Just tell yourself that their gremlin is out of control and walk away. It's the bravest and most confident thing you can do—it proves your maturity and intolerance for gremlin behavior.

RECAP: SELF-DOUBT? OH, IT'S JUST A LITTLE GREMLIN . . .

Self-doubt is a feeling of uncertainty about your abilities that can destroy your confidence. Think of it as an annoying, nagging gremlin full of drama and negativity.

But remember, self-doubt can never define your worth. Flick that gremlin off, show it who's boss, and let your confidence shine!

UNMASKING THE GREMLIN: WHAT CAUSES SELF-DOUBT?

Comparisonitis: the social media trap

Ever stumbled upon a photo of a classmate on a sunny beach, their carefree smile making you question why your life isn't as glamorous? Welcome to "comparisonitis," where social media feeds self-doubt. In this era of carefully curated highlight reels, it's natural to compare yourself to others. But remember, those filtered posts only reveal a fraction of the story.

How comparisonitis affects your self-esteem

In social psychology, there's a term called "upward social comparison." It refers to when you compare yourself to someone you perceive as better. For instance, you might look at the star athlete in your class and wonder why you're struggling to keep up while they ace every game. It can make you feel inadequate, like you're not measuring up.

Then there's "downward social comparison." This is when you compare yourself to someone you think is worse off than you. It's like looking at someone who doesn't do great in a school subject and thinking, "Well, at least I'm not as bad as them." It offers temporary relief, but it doesn't address your own insecurities.

Research shows that low self-esteem leads to more upward comparisons, trapping you in a cycle of feeling worse. However, not everyone ends up feeling down. Some use comparisons as motivation for self-improvement. It all depends on your perception of control and your belief in the possibility of change.

For example, imagine you're aspiring to be a faster runner, and you often compare yourself to the best runner you know. But instead of feeling inadequate, you feel inspired to learn from their technique. At the end of the day, it's all about channeling the comparison into positive growth.

How to handle comparisonitis

Don't be fooled by what you see online—those are just the highlight reels. In the real world, we all face hardships and doubts—even if our profiles suggest otherwise.

Comparing yourself to those picture-perfect snapshots is like comparing an unfinished puzzle to a finished one . . . It's simply not fair! There's a whole struggle involved in adjusting and moving all the pieces before anyone gets to see that brilliant picture at the end.

Instead of falling into the comparisonitis trap, reframe your thinking. Embrace your uniqueness, talents, passions, and experiences. Your journey is yours alone, and that's something to celebrate. Life isn't a competition; it's about embracing growth, progress, and individuality. So, the next time your pesky gremlin acts up, just tell it to shut up. Remind yourself that you're more than your online profile, and your classmates are more than theirs. Stop wasting energy on comparisons and redirect it toward self-acceptance, self-love, and celebrating your unique qualities.

Fear of failure: the "what if" game

There you are, minding your own business . . .

BAM!

An amazing idea pops into your head. It's the start of something huge, a dream waiting to burst into life. You can touch the excitement and passion bubbling inside you.

"But . . . What if everything goes horribly wrong and you fail?"

It's the self-doubt gremlin. Again.

Here's the thing about the gremlin: It's just trying to protect you. The human brain is wired to prioritize safety and comfort, so the fear of failure and the fear of the unknown often go hand in hand. There are times when the gremlin's response is actually valid. For example, if it warns you about not getting into a car with a random stranger, you should listen and get out of there.

But the gremlin has a problem—it can't tell the difference between danger and opportunity. It doesn't understand that playing it safe in every unfamiliar situation won't get you very far. Your job is to help the gremlin understand the difference.

Every successful person has faced failure at some point. Failure is as normal as breathing and should be viewed as a stepping stone toward growth and success. Just imagine if Thomas Edison had given up after his first few attempts at inventing the light bulb—we'd still be stumbling in the dark! He said:

> "I have not failed. I've just found 10,000 ways that won't work."

Instead of succumbing to the gremlin's "what ifs" and staying within your comfort zone, be bold. Challenge those doubts, explore your ideas, and pursue your dreams—even if it terrifies you. Take a deep breath, summon your courage, and make a promise to yourself that self-doubt won't control your destiny. Even if you stumble and fall, you'll learn invaluable lessons and uncover hidden strengths. Remember, failure is not the opposite of success; it's part of the journey.

In Chapter 3, we'll dive deeper into the anatomy of fear and talk about strategies to overcome it.

Negative influences: the dream snatchers

Picture this: You've overcome the fear of failure and now you're chasing your dreams like a boss. Next thing you know, you encounter someone who unintentionally blows a hole through your sails, forcing you to slow down or even halt.

Perhaps your friends question your abilities, or your parents express doubt about the feasibility of your dreams. It could also be the gremlin on your shoulder magnifying the doubts planted by others. Regardless, it feels like they're pelting little pebbles at your confidence, eroding it bit by bit.

Ouch, right?

Don't let them bring you down, though. We'll talk about how you can keep your head high in a bit, but first, let's talk about the two kinds of dream snatchers:

1. People with no interest in your success. They'll do and say anything to steer you off your course.
2. People who genuinely care about you but struggle to express their concerns in a supportive way.

Now, here's how to handle them: First and foremost, respect yourself enough to walk away from those who don't care. It may sound harsh, and it won't be easy, but it's the right and best decision. You'll never need the first type of dream snatcher. They'll only drain your positive energy and label you a coward. Let. Them. Go.

Surround yourself with positive, uplifting people who believe in you. This isn't about seeking validation or permission to pursue your dreams. It's about finding your tribe—the people who will cheer you on when you feel discouraged or distracted.

Dealing with the second type of dream snatcher is trickier, because they don't intend to put you down, and they honestly care about you. It's your responsibility to explain to them that their negativity isn't helpful. That said, remain open to their concerns and consider whether they might have a valid point. Perhaps their lack of support stems from how you're approaching your dreams rather than the dreams themselves. Just be willing to engage in conversations. Remember, confidence is not arrogance.

You're the captain of your own ship, sailing through the vast ocean of life. Stormy seas and rough waves may come your way, but you have the power to navigate your course. Never allow the dream snatchers to grab the steering wheel and change your trajectory. Take control, steer confidently, and sail toward your dreams with determination.

Past experiences

Negative past experiences are like tiny seeds of self-doubt. They take root in your mind and make you question your ability to succeed. It could be the memory of that test you studied hard for but didn't quite ace, the unintentional hurt you caused a friend, or the embarrassment and rejection you faced after pouring your heart into something.

Although it may not feel like it now, your past experiences don't have the power to define your future. They're simply part of the journey. Just because you faced setbacks in the past doesn't mean you're bound for failure. Remember what Thomas Edison said about finding 10,000 ways that didn't work? In your life, you'll encounter numerous paths that lead to dead ends, too, but that's just life. The trick is to persist and believe in yourself.

It's kind of like encountering a tough level in a video game: Every time you get knocked down, you don't give up, but you learn from your mistakes, adjust your strategy, and come back stronger every time until you push through. Every experience, good or bad, holds lessons and opportunities for growth. All you have to do is believe in your ability to learn and overcome any obstacle.

Embrace the ghosts of the past as friendly reminders of how far you've come and let them inspire you to keep pushing forward. You've got this!

Unrealistic expectations: the perfection trap

Setting unrealistic expectations for yourself is an open invitation for self-doubt. It can lead to disappointment and frustration.

The worst part about pursuing perfection? It's an illusion. It's like chasing the source of a rainbow. No matter how hard you try, you'll never attain that elusive state of flawlessness. And you know what? That's perfectly OK!

Who said life had to be flawless anyway? We're here to live, experience, and navigate through obstacles on our path to self-discovery. It's the detours and unexpected twists that give our lives meaning and provide unforgettable stories. Have you ever heard someone say, "Let me tell you about that time when everything in my life was perfect . . ."? It's unlikely, and even thinking about it might make you yawn with boredom.

Instead of fixating on perfection, shift your focus to progress. Life is a journey of growth, and every small step forward is worth celebrating. Whether it's acing a quiz, finishing a project, or mustering up the courage to try something new, every victory deserves recognition.

Stop setting unrealistic expectations for yourself and stop thinking your friends, parents, teachers, or mentors expect perfection from you. They don't. They only expect you to do your best—and there's a massive difference.

Give your all in everything you do and relish in the joy of progress. Nurture your skills, talents, and confidence. Yes, there will be setbacks and stumbles along the way, but keep going. With time and effort, you'll realize that realistic expectations mixed with mistakes are far more rewarding than unrealistic expectations that lead to nothing.

Embrace the messiness that comes with growth and aim to become the best version of yourself without striving for perfection —it doesn't exist!

RECAP: DODGE THE SELF-DOUBT TRIGGERS THAT FEED THE PESKY GREMLIN

Remember Professor Snape from Harry Potter? Now there's a guy who could cause some serious self-doubt, right? Whenever you want to recall the causes of self-doubt, just think of Professor Snape:

S: Social media comparisonitis: the trap of comparing yourself to others.

N: Navigate the "what if" game by overcoming your fear of failure.

A: Avoid negative influences by dealing with dream snatchers.

P: Past experiences can never define your future.

E: Embrace realistic expectations and escape the perfection trap.

THE LINK BETWEEN YOUR EARLY CHILDHOOD EXPERIENCES, YOUR SELF-ESTEEM, AND YOUR CONFIDENCE

Think of your early childhood as the prologue to the epic tale of your life. How you were raised plays a significant role in shaping your confidence.

If you received love, support, and encouragement during your early years, it laid the foundation for a strong sense of self-worth and fortified you against self-doubt and insecurity. Conversely, if you had limited opportunities or a lack of support and encouragement, it likely made you more vulnerable to the self-doubt gremlin's influence—leading to lower self-esteem and confidence.

Just like tree seeds can germinate and take root wherever the wind blows them, we humans have no control over the circumstances we're born into. However, unlike trees, we have the incredible potential to make things work out in our favor, no matter what our early experiences were. You're the captain of your own ship, and you have the power to change course toward a life filled with high self-esteem and boundless confidence.

	SELF-ESTEEM	CONFIDENCE
Definition	It's equal to how much you value yourself as a person overall and determines how much you believe you're worthy of friendship, love, and recognition.	An unwavering self-belief in your abilities, potential, and social savviness (see epistemic and social confidence in Chapter 1).
Example	"I deserve respect and love because I'm pretty awesome in my own unique way!"	"I can totally do this thing!"
Relationship	Having high self-esteem can give you a boost of confidence in different areas. When you feel worthy, you're more likely to take risks and face challenges with a positive attitude.	If you lack confidence in something, it can chip away at your self-esteem. Doubts and negative thoughts can creep in, making you question your worth.
Interplay	When your self-esteem is low, it can be tough to build confidence. You might doubt yourself and feel unworthy of success. It's a real struggle.	At the same time, not having confidence in certain areas can bring down your self-esteem. It's like a cycle where one affects the other.
Importance	Self-esteem is like the foundation of how you see yourself as a whole. It affects your self-image, self-acceptance, and emotional well-being. It's a big deal!	Confidence is essential for taking action, going after goals, and overcoming challenges. It helps you grow personally and succeed in different areas of life.

Let's explore some practical tips that can help you change your course.

Reflect on your self-worth: Recognize your unique strengths, abilities, and potential. Celebrate your accomplishments, no matter how small, and remind yourself daily that you are enough and worthy.

Set achievable goals: If you have big dreams, good for you! But sometimes, a big dream can feel overwhelming and seem impossible to achieve. Break it down into smaller, manageable goals. Taking consistent action and making progress will cultivate a sense of accomplishment and boost your confidence.

Practice self-care and self-compassion: Prioritize activities that bring you joy, help you relax, and nourish your soul. Get enough exercise, sleep well, eat healthy foods, and feed your mind with good stuff. Practice positive self-talk and embrace your imperfections with compassion.

Explore your interests and develop your skills: Invest time in activities that ignite your passion. Whether it's a hobby, sport, art, music, or academic pursuit, focusing on something you love will provide a sense of purpose and contribute to your confidence.

Ask for support: Seeking help is not a sign of weakness but a courageous and wise choice. If you find it challenging to boost your self-esteem on your own, reach out to a trusted adult for guidance and support.

RECAP: WHERE YOU COME FROM DOESN'T DEFINE WHERE YOU'RE GOING

While your early childhood experiences may have influenced your self-esteem and confidence, you have control over how you develop them moving forward. Invest in your interests, set achievable goals, be mindful of self-doubt triggers, and don't hesitate to seek support from a trusted adult if needed.

You've got this!

END-OF-CHAPTER ACTIVITY: TAKE THE HELM, CAPTAIN!

In the above section, you learned about practical ways to change the course of your confidence-development journey. No matter the foundation you received during your early childhood, you'll always deal with people and situations that challenge your self-esteem and confidence. This activity will help you stay your course in the face of those challenges.

Ready? Grab a pen and notebook and let's do this.

Step 1: Highlight your strengths.
Think of three things about yourself that you're really good at or proud of. It could be anything from being an amazing friend, acing that one subject in school, or even that secret skill you use to impress people! Take a second to jot them down.

Step 2: Highlight your current challenges.
Write down the top three challenges you're facing right now. Maybe it's dealing with school stress, making new friends, or trying something you've never done before. Don't worry; we all have our share of things we have to deal with!

Step 3: Reframe your challenges.

This is the fun part. Imagine that those challenges are actually opportunities to show off your strengths. For example, if you're nervous about trying something new and one of your strengths is being an amazing friend, think about how you would encourage your friend to be brave.

Step 4: Visualize your confidence.

Imagine yourself as someone who has already conquered your self-doubt and visualize an outcome where you have overcome all three of your challenges. Can you feel the self-esteem and confidence emanating from you? Powerful stuff, right? It's totally within your reach.

Step 5: Take SMART steps to conquer all your challenges from now on.

Now that you know challenges are just opportunities in disguise and that it's possible to reframe them, that's exactly what you should do from now on. But don't just see the opportunity—set a SMART goal for yourself to conquer it:

Specific (clear and well defined)
Measurable (it should be easy to track from start to finish)
Achievable (realistic and attainable)
Relevant (align with your values and objectives)
Time-bound (have a deadline)

With this formula, you'll be truly in control of your life and be able to live with clarity, direction, and unshakable self-esteem and confidence.

Now that you understand the roots of self-doubt, it's time to dissect the biggest culprit behind it: fear. If you can, be sure to complete the above activity before you dive into Chapter 3.

Reminder: If you ever need a refresher on anything we talked about in this chapter, head over to the *Recap* part of each section.

See you on the other side!

CHAPTER 3
THE ANATOMY OF FEAR (EXPLORING SELF-DOUBT PART 2)

"Fear is a powerful emotion, but it's not a permanent one."

SUSAN JEFFERS

THE FUNDAMENTALS

Fear is your body's alarm system. Whenever you sense trouble or danger, it kicks in and tells you to do something about it. Imagine having to do something you hate. Whether it's giving a presentation, participating in a social or sports activity, or something your family expects you to do, your alarm system will typically kick in right before the event takes place. It will bombard you with a racing heart, shallow breathing, sweaty palms and armpits, and a barrage of "what if" thoughts. Then, just as you're about to take part in the activity, you'll have one of two reactions:

1. The "fight" response: You'll take a deep breath, try to calm yourself, and proceed with the activity, or
2. The "flight" response: You'll freeze, feel too overwhelmed, and not take part in the activity.

Conversely, there's anxiety—that nagging, uneasy feeling that makes you worry about things that may or may not happen. For example, before a big presentation, you might worry about tripping on stage, stumbling over your words, or making a blunder that will become the talk of the school.

While those are all possible scenarios, they're very unlikely to happen. And that's the thing about anxiety . . . ninety-nine times out of a hundred, people end up worrying about nothing because all the wild scenarios their minds imagine never happen. Even so, anxiety has the power to amplify fear like it's nobody's business.

Have a look at the table below to get a better idea of the difference between fear and anxiety, as well as the delicate interplay between the two:

	FEAR	ANXIETY	INTERPLAY
Definition	Your response to a specific and immediate threat or danger.	Your response to a vague and often imagined "what if" scenario.	Fear can trigger anxiety, while anxiety can amplify fear.
Examples	Being chased by a stray dog. Getting startled by a sudden loud noise. Fear of heights while standing in a tall building. Seeing the school bully approach you.	Feeling stressed over the upcoming exams. Worrying about social interactions and making friends (social anxiety). Racing thoughts and difficulty concentrating. Feeling restless and on the edge for no specific reason.	Your fear of failing an exam can trigger anxiety. Social anxiety can lead to the fear of being judged by others. Anxiety can cause an overall fear of losing control and a fear of failure.
How fear influences anxiety and vice versa	Fear can trigger a temporary anxiety response to prepare your body to fight or flee under normal circumstances. However, anxiety can make your fear reactions worse and make them more persistent and more intense. Left unchecked, anxiety can lower your threshold for fear responses, making everyday situations more threatening.		

HOW ANXIETY AFFECTS YOU

While anxiety is totally normal, it can interfere with your life if it gets out of control, so it's important to manage it. Training your mind to be calmer will make your responses to fear less severe and help you develop a higher fear threshold. This means you'll redefine what you perceive as threatening or dangerous (but don't do a Nala and go laughing in the face of really serious stuff, OK?).

Here's why you don't want anxiety to get out of control, like *ever* . . .

Anxiety can mess with your school life. When you're anxious, it's harder to concentrate, remember things, and make important choices. This can discourage you from doing schoolwork and make you avoid your education altogether.

Anxiety can mess with your social life, too. Worrying about being judged or rejected can make it hard to make friends, join group activities, and socialize. This, in turn, can make you feel isolated and increase your anxiety.

Anxiety can take you on an emotional ride, making you feel overwhelmed, angry, and frustrated. This heightened state makes it nearly impossible to relax and enjoy life because you're always on edge.

Anxiety can cause headaches, stomachaches, tense muscles, fatigue, and keep you up at night. As if that's not bad enough, it can weaken your immune system, making you more susceptible to illnesses or worsening existing health conditions.

Sometimes, when anxiety gets too overwhelming, it can **make people turn to dangerous "solutions."** Drugs and alcohol may seem like quick fixes, but in the long run, they can create worse problems.

Anxiety can strain family relations. It can lead to breakdowns in communication and cause conflict, confusion, and frustration for everyone.

If you don't address anxiety now, it can stalk you into adulthood and cause more problems. Living with unchecked anxiety can limit your personal growth, deprive you of opportunities, and make you unhappy. Eventually, it can lead to more serious issues like depression or substance abuse.

UNDERSTANDING FEAR-BASED BEHAVIOR

How fear influences your behavior

Everyone knew Hannah as a fearless person. They looked up to her because she loved leading projects, speaking in front of others, and challenging her comfort zone. But she had a secret: She was afraid of water slides, and the mere thought of sliding down that colossal structure sent shivers down her spine.

One day, she had to face her fear while hanging out with her friends at the theme park. While everyone's laughter and excitement filled the air, Hannah's heart raced, and she felt an intense shortness of breath. Her self-doubt gremlin whispered in her ear, conjuring images of embarrassment, loss of control, and potential harm. It had a firm hold on her, suffocating her natural desire for fun and adventure.

Hannah watched as her friends soared down the water slide one by one, their cheers fading into the distance. The battle inside her intensified as the fear urged her to retreat and come up with excuses to avoid the challenge.

Hannah's fear of water slides may not be too serious, but let's examine the real issue: She knows everyone looks up to her because she's the brave one. So, maybe Hanna's deeper fear is losing her friends because they'll think she's a fraud when she doesn't take risks. And just because of that, she might go down the water slide. In this case, facing her fear would be a good thing, because she'll challenge her comfort zone and learn more about herself in a healthy way.

But what about next time?

How far would Hannah be willing to go to "prove" she's not a fraud? If, for example, her friends want to experiment with alcohol or drugs and she has no interest in doing so, will she cave in because she believes she's supposed to be the brave one?

Do you see how fear can influence your behavior? It can push you to take dangerous risks that compromise your values and well-being. In Chapter 7, we'll chat about how to overcome this kind of pressure.

Signs that fear is a hindrance in your life

Think of specific aspects of your life while reading through the below tell-tales. For example, you may think you're just determined to do your best in everything, but are you perhaps overdoing it in sports or academics to the extent that you're afraid of failing?

- You set impossible standards for yourself and feel like a failure when you don't reach them.
- You're settling for less than what you want in life.
- You say yes to things you should say no to, and vice versa.
- You have trouble speaking up and setting boundaries.
- You put things off until the last minute.
- You're a master at finding distractions to keep you busy so you can avoid projects and tasks.

The above behaviors are all associated with the most common worst fears teenagers deal with. We'll zoom in on those fears (and how to overcome them) in the 'How to overcome your worst fears' section.

How you react to fear and trauma

As a teen, you're not only dealing with fear, but you're also transitioning from childhood to adulthood. This is a particularly challenging time of your life, and sometimes you'll feel like things are out of control. That's normal. As long as you bounce back after setbacks and believe in yourself, you're doing just fine. Let's look at some ways you might react to fear and traumatic experiences:

- You'll experience an emotional roller coaster of sadness, anger, anxiety, and guilt, which can sometimes leave you feeling like you're stuck in a loop-de-loop.
- You may feel the urge to withdraw from family and friends when bad things happen. Taking some alone time can be helpful, but remember, reaching out for support is crucial too.
- Fear can make you react in unexpected ways such as acting out, rebelling, or giving up responsibilities. It's also possible to lose interest in things you used to enjoy. These are all part of your self-discovery journey. That said, if your acting out leads to trouble, or if nothing interests you for weeks or months, you should ask a trusted adult for help.
- Fear can make you pessimistic, cynical, and distrustful of others. It might even affect your memory, concentration, and problem-solving abilities. Don't worry, though—your mind is powerful and with time and support, you'll regain your mental ninja skills.

Remember, there is zero shame in telling your parents, a trusted teacher, or a mentor what you're going through. Even if you can't articulate it well, they'll feel honored that you went to them and will do their best to help you through your tough patch.

How to know when you're acting out of fear

- Pay attention to your body. It's like your personal fear-o-meter. If your heart starts racing, your palms get sweaty, or your stomach does somersaults, it's probably fear talking.
- If you catch yourself constantly doubting yourself or putting yourself down, fear is probably the culprit in your inner monologue.

- Are you avoiding situations or challenges because they make you feel uneasy? Fear often tells you to run and hide, but remember, facing them instead can lead to incredible personal growth.
- Trust your instincts. If something feels off, it could be fear warning you of real danger. Take a moment to pause, breathe, and listen to that gut feeling.

You've got the power to face your fears head-on and create a life filled with courage and resilience, but fear-based behavior can be a hurdle. Recognizing when you're acting out of fear is the first step to taking back control.

HOW TO OVERCOME YOUR WORST FEARS

This section may not address *all* the fears that are stealing your joy and holding you back, but it talks about the ones I'm almost 100% sure are gnawing at your confidence. I say "almost" because I'm not a mind reader (although my kids think I am sometimes!). It's just that I have a good idea because, through the ages, teenagers have struggled with a handful of common fears—myself, my siblings, all our old classmates, and your parents included.

If you can learn to overcome these common fears at this critical stage of your life, nothing will stand in your way.

THE FEAR OF NOT MEETING EXPECTATIONS

It feels like the entire world expects you to be a straight-A student, right? But, seriously, you're so much more than just your grades. This fear is linked to the pursuit of perfection. But you already know perfection is a game no one can win, so stop yourself before you get sucked into a frustrating cycle. Here are some practical tips:

Set realistic goals: Identify your areas of interest and focus on improving in those while maintaining a balanced approach to your other responsibilities.

Acknowledge your efforts: Even if outcomes don't match your expectations, take pride in your dedication and hard work.

Embrace mistakes as learning opportunities: Reframe your mistakes as valuable learning experiences. Analyze them, identify areas for improvement, and use them as stepping stones toward success.

Develop effective study habits: Create a structured study plan that allows you to manage your time efficiently. Break down large tasks into smaller, manageable steps, and prioritize your workload accordingly.

THE FEAR OF HOW OTHERS PERCEIVE YOU (SOCIAL ANXIETY)

We all want to fit in and have friends who appreciate us for who we are. But sometimes, our minds can create scary scenarios, telling us what other people must be thinking. It's like our brains are a little too creative for their own good.

Most of the time, though, the things you imagine aren't true. Trust me, people aren't sitting around judging you 24/7. They're too busy worrying about their own lives, what to wear tomorrow, or what's for lunch (or perhaps fighting their own social anxiety). Apply the following tips to overcome your social anxiety:

Embrace your uniqueness: Rock your quirks, talents, and your passions. Be proud of who you are and let that confidence shine through.

Start small: Social confidence doesn't happen in a snap. Begin by engaging in conversations with people you're comfortable with.

Practice active listening, making eye contact, and asking questions.

Challenge your negative thoughts: Instead of assuming the worst, ask yourself, "What's the evidence for this thought? Is it really true?" Most fears are based on assumptions rather than facts. Replace those negative thoughts with positive ones, like "I am worthy of friendship," or "I have interesting things to say."

Practice, practice, practice: Like any skill, socializing takes practice. Join clubs or organizations or teams where you can meet people who share your interests. The more you interact with others, the more comfortable you'll become. Remember, it's okay to stumble or feel awkward at first. We all do!

Be kind to yourself: Don't beat yourself up if you feel nervous or make a social blunder. Remember that you're growing and learning, so treat yourself with kindness and compassion—just as you would a close friend who's going through a rough patch.

THE FEAR OF REJECTION

Rejection is a part of life. It happens to everyone, even the coolest, most popular people you know. But never forget: Opinions don't define worth. Here are some practical tips to beat the fear of rejection:

Embrace your inner bravery: Challenge yourself to do something that scares you a little every day—even if it's something small. The more you flex your brave muscles, the stronger they get.

Flip the script on rejection: Instead of viewing rejection as a personal blow, reframe it as a learning opportunity. Ask yourself, "What can I learn from this experience?" Maybe there's a fresh approach you can try next time. It's all about growth and resilience, and every rejection brings you closer to your goals.

Surround yourself with support: The friends you already have are your support squad. Share your goals and fears with them and let them cheer you on. They'll be there to lift you up when you're feeling down and remind you of your awesomeness.

Prepare for the possibilities: Before taking a chance, do a little homework. Whether it's asking someone out or going for an opportunity, gather some information and come up with a game plan. By preparing yourself, you'll boost your confidence and increase your chances of a positive outcome.

Be true to you: Never change who you are or what you believe in just to get someone's stamp of approval. Stay confident in who you are—the world will notice, and the right people will want to be your friends.

THE FEAR OF CRITICISM, THE FEAR OF GOSSIP, THE FEAR OF EMBARRASSMENT

THE FEAR OF CRITICISM

No matter how fantastic you are, there will always be critics out there. It's like they have a degree in nitpicking or something, right? Again, people's opinions don't define you. Here's what you can do to fight this fear:

Welcome constructive criticism: When someone offers feedback, take a deep breath, and listen with an open mind. Separate the helpful nuggets from the unnecessary negativity. Remember, even the most accomplished people have room for improvement.

Focus on self-acceptance: The most important opinion of you should come from . . . you! Recognize your strengths, celebrate your achievements, and learn from your mistakes. When you believe in yourself, the critics' voices are just faint blah-blah-blahs.

THE FEAR OF GOSSIP

Negative rumors are bad news for anyone's confidence. While there's no foolproof way to avoid it, you can definitely do a few things to overcome this fear while minimizing your chances of becoming the victim of gossip. Let's see what they are:

Mind your own business: Focus on being the best version of yourself instead of getting tangled up in other people's drama. Channel your energy into positive pursuits and let the gossip monkeys swing elsewhere.

Choose your tribe wisely: Surround yourself with friends who respect your boundaries and have your back. A good friend won't engage in gossip or spread rumors about you or others.

Lead by example: Instead of joining the rumor mill, lead with kindness and empathy. If someone tries to gossip in your presence, put your foot down and show that spreading positivity is way cooler than stirring up drama.

THE FEAR OF EMBARRASSMENT

Ah, the fear of becoming a walking, talking meme. Everyone has an awkward moment now and then. Ask your siblings or parents —it should be a fun conversation. Here's a story of what happened to me:

One day, I was visiting a friend's house, and her mom asked me what I was planning on majoring in when I went to college.

"I'd love to be an English major," I said, "but I'm not sure what career options are available for that."

My friend's mom replied, "Well, you could be a librarian!"

"Haha! Very funny . . . Who would do that?" I asked self-assured.

She just looked at me and said, "I'm a librarian."

Yep. I felt pretty humiliated. My friend's mom was a good sport and laughed it off and everything was fine, but I was incredibly embarrassed!

If (and when) something awkward happens to you, the key is basically going with the flow and not allowing that moment to haunt you forever. Here are some practical tips to overcome the fear of embarrassment:

Embrace your inner goofball: Life's too short to take everything seriously, so trip over your shoelaces and snort while laughing with pride. Remember, laughter is contagious, and being able to laugh at yourself is a gift that will serve you well for life.

Reframe embarrassment as growth: Every embarrassing moment is a chance to grow and learn. Instead of replaying the cringe-worthy scene in your head, ask yourself, "What can I take away from this? How can I handle a similar situation better next time?"

Use these moments as stepping stones to become a more confident and resilient version of yourself.

THE FEAR OF THE UNKNOWN

Fear of the unknown is like standing at a crossroads and feeling uneasy about which path to take. It's natural to feel a little anxious or hesitant. Your brain likes to stick to what's familiar and predictable, and it will try to steer you away from the unknown without even considering that something incredibly exciting might be around the corner. Here's what you can do to feel less afraid of the unknown:

Embrace the thrill of the unexpected: Life would be pretty dull if we always knew what was coming next. So, shift your mindset from fear to excitement and let curiosity be your compass.

Expand your comfort zone with baby steps: Take small steps outside of what's familiar to make the unknown feel less terrifying. Maybe it's trying a new hobby, exploring a different genre of music, or joining a club or group that piques your interest.

Adopt the growth mindset: Whether or not your brain likes it, the unknown is where growth happens. Nurture the belief that you can develop your abilities through dedication and hard work and use challenges as opportunities. With a growth mindset, you'll always come out stronger and wiser (and have an epic story to tell).

Find comfort in the present moment: Often, the fear of the unknown stems from worrying about the future. Shift your attention to being present and making the most of each moment. When you're fully engaged in the present, the unknown becomes a little less daunting.

RECAP: CONQUER YOUR WORST FEARS LIKE A BOSS

Worried about not meeting expectations?

- Set realistic goals.
- Embrace mistakes.
- Develop good study habits.

Social anxiety bothering you?

- Remember, people aren't that focused on you because they've got their own stuff going on.
- Embrace your uniqueness.
- Challenge negative thoughts.
- Practice being social.
- Be kind to yourself.

Fear of rejection?

- Embrace bravery.
- Learn from rejections.
- Surround yourself with support.
- Stay true to yourself.

Afraid of criticism, gossip, and embarrassment?

- Embrace constructive criticism.
- Focus on self-acceptance.
- Mind your own business.
- Choose good friends.
- Lead by example.
- Embrace your inner goofball.
- Reframe embarrassment as growth.

Scared of the unknown?

- Embrace the thrill.

- Conquer your comfort zone with baby steps.
- Ask yourself: "Why not?"
- Embrace a growth mindset.
- Find comfort in the present.

THE CONNECTION BETWEEN FEAR AND SELF-DOUBT

John, the school's star tennis player, had a creative side that only his family, closest friends, and a trusted teacher at school knew about. The teacher convinced John that his classmates would be inspired to try new things if they knew about his passion. Eventually, John agreed to hold a solo art exhibition at the school's annual arts and crafts expo. He poured everything into creating his paintings and had immense fun doing it. However, as the expo date approached, he experienced a mix of emotions.

The night before the exhibition, John felt a sense of dread creeping in. He was worried about what his classmates might think of his art and whether they would appreciate his work. Fear made him anxious about receiving criticism and being rejected. He questioned his artistic abilities and talent, comparing himself to more established artists and telling himself he should rather stick to tennis. But soon after, he started doubting whether he was a good enough tennis player, too. He felt like a fraud.

Although distinct, fear and self-doubt often go hand in hand, and they can really interfere with your confidence and happiness. Let's see how they connect:

Fear can affect your self-belief: It can make you wonder if you're capable or good enough to handle challenges. The pesky gremlin may act up and say things like "You can't do this, you'll mess up!" The less you believe in yourself, the more these feelings can take over.

Self-doubt makes fear even scarier: When you already doubt yourself, fear can feel much worse. In turn, the fear intensifies your self-doubt and creates a vicious cycle that breaks down your self-esteem.

It makes dealing with life harder: When fear and self-doubt hit, you might try to avoid challenges altogether, procrastinate, or seek constant reassurance from others to feel better temporarily.

Excessive fear and self-doubt are both confidence killers and common obstacles to success in life, but both can be overcome with a positive mindset. Yes, developing a positive mindset is easier said than done, but with deliberate practice, the shift happens way faster than you think (we'll talk more about developing a better mindset in Chapters 4 and 5).

RECAP: WHAT'S THE CONNECTION BETWEEN FEAR AND SELF-DOUBT?

Fear and self-doubt sometimes team up to sabotage your confidence and happiness. Fear makes you doubt yourself, while self-doubt intensifies the fear. By cultivating a positive mindset, you can break this cycle and overcome these confidence killers, increasing your chances of success and happiness by a long shot.

END-OF-CHAPTER ACTIVITY: BEAT FEAR AND ANXIETY BEFORE THEY BEAT YOU

Step 1: Identify your fears and anxieties.
Take a few moments to reflect on your own fears and anxieties. Write down at least three specific fears or situations that make you anxious. These could be related to school,

social interactions, personal goals, or anything else that comes to mind.

Step 2: Think about where they come from.
Try to identify the root cause behind the fears and anxieties you've listed. Are you afraid of failing or being judged? Does the idea of rejection send chills down your spine? Or perhaps you hate thinking about the unknown . . .
Whatever it is, understanding why these things bother you so much may give you a whole new point of view. You may realize they're rooted in some simple incident that happened like forever ago. You may even discover you've been feeding yourself a bunch of lies over a TV series or movie you watched recently.
This step can help you see the truth behind a lot of things you think are real threats or issues. But if you don't feel better afterward, or if you managed to only get one or two fears out of the way, move on to the next step.

Step 3: Ask yourself: "What's the absolute worst that can happen if this fear comes true?"
So, maybe your fear has a REAL possibility of coming true. In that case, imagine for a moment that it does happen. One moment everything is fine and then suddenly that thing you've been dreading becomes reality. Your best friend has rejected you, the entire class is laughing at you, you weren't chosen for the team after all your hard work, or [think of your listed fears].
Now, ask yourself, "What's the worst thing that can happen now that my fear has come true?"
Jot down the possible outcomes.
If your best friend rejected you, some people may talk and stare. Maybe your ex-friend starts spreading rumors about you.
If you embarrassed yourself in front of the entire class, it

may stick with you for a while. Bullies may make fun of you, or the story can spread like wildfire to the rest of the school.

Take a deep breath and take a good look at those possibilities. Let them sink in. Imagine it's as real as real can get. Now, say this out loud: "I accept that these things can happen, and if they do, I'll survive. I'll be ready. But I'll never allow it to defeat me. Never."

You see, when you imagine the worst outcome and accept it in your mind before it even happens, something mind-blowing happens. First, the idea of it doesn't bother you as much anymore, and second, in the very, very, very (very!) rare case that it actually happens, it's not going to break your stride one bit. You'll hit the ground running from whatever height or angle you fall and simply move on with envy-worthy confidence.

BUT . . . this isn't the end of the story. You have the power to minimize the chances of worst-case scenarios to almost zero. Let's see how!

Step 4: Create a fear-busting action plan.
You know what you're afraid of and you know where it comes from. Now it's time to (1) think about what you can do to prevent it from happening, and (2) think about your game plan if it happens.

Come up with a preventative plan:
There's no set-in-stone formula to follow because each fear is unique. Your mission is to analyze each fear on its own merits and then brainstorm ways to prevent it from happening.

For example, if you fear being rejected by your best friend, you probably need to have a heart-to-heart in the mirror. Why would they reject you? Do they expect you to do things you're not comfortable with? Is your friendship dependent on you doing these things? And if that's the case, are they really your friend, or can you do better? On the other hand, if you know your friendship is solid, then maybe you should have a chat with your friend. Tell them you have this crazy idea in your head that this thing can happen, why you're afraid of it, and what you think the consequences might be. Your friend can probably do an excellent job at helping you put this fear to rest.

Come up with an in-case-of-emergency game plan:
If your fear comes true, what are the next steps you'll take? For example, if you have a fear of embarrassing yourself in front of the class, think of ways you can turn the situation around in your favor if it should happen. Maybe you should be the one to make the first joke. Maybe train your mind not to react in a way that will make you look hurt and humiliated—if bullies can't see that they're hitting nerves, you take all their ammunition away.

Step 5: Immortalize your progress.
Keep a journal or a confidence diary where you record how you're overcoming your fears and anxieties. Write about your successes AND your setbacks, as well as the lessons you learn along the way. Finally, refer back to your entries often to remind yourself of your growth and resilience.

Now that you're armed with the knowledge of what self-doubt is, how it relates to fear, and know how to overcome it, you'll start spreading confidence vibes like never before.

But there's even more confidence to gain and more fun to be had! Head over to the next chapter to learn what self-awareness is, why it matters, and how to cultivate an unstoppable positive mindset.

THE POWER OF ONE VOICE

"When you have confidence, you can have a lot of fun. And when you have fun, you can do amazing things."

JOE NAMATH

Do you remember the story I told you in the introduction about the old man on the bench? I remember that moment years and years later, and the whole interaction couldn't have lasted longer than about five minutes.

A total stranger sharing his wisdom had that much impact on me. It's true that I had a lot to learn to gain that confidence he was talking about, but that one small conversation lodged in the back of my mind and boosted me on my journey toward finding it.

One voice can make a huge difference, and that's the reason I became a teacher. I knew I could help, and I've seen that to be true–not least as my students have grown in confidence. In fact, if I'm honest, it's in watching their confidence grow that I find the most satisfaction in knowing that I had an impact–more so than in the subject knowledge I teach.

But you don't need to be a teacher to make an impact in this way. Just a few sentences from you can have enormous power–just like those uttered by the man I met in the park.

You can help someone like you on their own journey to grow their confidence and settle into their true selves simply by pointing them in the direction of this book… and that can be done without even leaving the comfort of your own room.

By leaving a review of this book on Amazon, you'll show other young people that there's hope for them too, and you'll point them in the direction of the guidance that will help them become the confident person they long to be.

Simply by letting other readers know how this book has helped you and what they'll find inside, you'll not only show them that it's possible for them to grow their confidence; you'll lead them straight to the resource that will help them get there.

Thank you for your support. Every voice counts – including yours.

CHAPTER 4
BUILDING SELF-AWARENESS

> "Look outside and you will see yourself. Look inside and you will find yourself."

> DREW GERALD

Dear Diary,

Today was mind-blowing! So, I met this boy named Bailey. There I was, minding my own business, when I saw him looking super depressed. I don't know what got into me, but I went up to him and asked if he needed company.

Listening to Bailey's story was like looking into a mirror! The stuff he shared was eerily similar to my own struggles, you know? But here's the crazy part: Just by being there for him, I discovered this hidden strength within myself—I'm actually a good listener. Who knew, right? And seeing Bailey's relief and gratitude was pretty awesome. Kindness goes such a long way . . . But I think it's about more than just helping others; it actually helps you learn about yourself.

Until next time!

WHAT IS SELF-AWARENESS?

Self-awareness means understanding your own actions, thoughts, and feelings really well. It's this amazing ability to look at yourself objectively and from a different perspective.

There are two types of self-awareness: One is about how you appear to others (public self-awareness), and the other is about understanding your inner thoughts and emotions (private self-awareness).

Being self-aware helps you in many ways, including:

- It gives you the power to influence outcomes in your life.
- You know what's right for you and make better decisions.
- You communicate with clarity and confidence.
- You have an open mind and understand different points of view.
- You act with fairness and understanding because you avoid making assumptions.
- You build better relationships because you can understand others' feelings better.
- You handle your emotions better.

Here's the cool part—self-awareness isn't some static thing we're all born with. As with building confidence, you can become more self-aware, and in this chapter, we'll chat about how you can build self-awareness and why it matters.

THE LINK BETWEEN SELF-AWARENESS AND CONFIDENCE

To really appreciate the link between self-awareness and confidence, let's revisit the definition of confidence:

• • •

Confidence means believing in your abilities and embracing your individuality. When you're confident, you act on your beliefs and always push through when things get tough, no matter what. To build confidence, you need to practice a confident mindset every day (BEAPP up!).

Now, imagine not knowing yourself. You're not sure what you believe in, and you can't really pinpoint what you're good at. If confidence means believing in yourself and your abilities, but you don't know what they are, how can you become more confident?

That's where self-awareness comes in. It's the secret sauce you need to fuel your confidence.

Have you ever seen those incredible athletes who excel at their sport? They know their bodies inside out. They know their strengths, like lightning-fast speed or killer accuracy, but they also know their weaknesses, like maybe not being the tallest player on the field. With all that insider information, those athletes can play to their strengths and strategize around their limitations.

That's self-awareness in action!

It's like having your own user manual that gives you a rundown of your strengths, weaknesses, passions, and values. Not to mention the cool insights into what makes you tick, what makes you feel alive, and what makes you feel like you're in the zone. How could you *not* feel confident if you know so much about yourself?

And when you know yourself well, you naturally love yourself more—quirks and all. Ultimately, self-awareness turns you into a force to be reckoned with. You radiate confidence because you know who you are, what you stand for, and where you're headed.

How self-awareness builds confidence

When you know what you're good at and where you can improve, you can make smarter choices and set realistic goals for yourself. When you achieve them, you'll be rewarded with sweet confidence.

When you're self-aware, you're also more in tune with your values, passions, and beliefs. You know what truly matters to you, what sets your soul on fire, and what makes you unique. This deep understanding of yourself gives you a sense of purpose and direction, which makes you a more confident human.

Self-awareness is also about recognizing your quirks, insecurities, and areas where you can grow. We all have those, trust me! Being aware of your weaknesses puts you at an advantage because you can come up with strategies to overcome them and avoid awkward situations.

With self-awareness comes the power to say yes or no to new experiences on your own terms. You can make choices that align with your values and stay true to yourself, all while being mindful of how your decisions and actions impact those around you.

RECAP: WHAT IS SELF-AWARENESS AND WHY DOES IT MATTER?

Self-awareness means knowing yourself inside out. It's like having a mirror that shows you exactly who you are. Self-awareness matters because it's the secret to confidence, and you can't be a confident human if you don't know yourself.

SELF-REFLECTION AND MINDFULNESS: THE ULTIMATE MAP TO SELF-AWARENESS

What is self-reflection?

It's a fantastic, sunny day, and the math class is in high spirits. Rudy had just answered a question from the teacher, and now it's Callie's turn. She gets it wrong, but the teacher patiently explains the equation again and asks Callie to try again. Out of nowhere, Callie breaks down. She yells at the teacher, slams her book shut, and storms out of the class, leaving everyone perplexed.

Have you ever seen or experienced a similar situation? What happened to Callie isn't uncommon. In fact, even adults can have meltdowns like that. While the daily grind of life gets to all of us, there's something deeper going on here, and it has to do with how well Callie knows herself. She might think things over later and ask herself questions like:

- *Why did I react that way?*
- *What thoughts and emotions triggered my outburst?*
- *What could I have done differently?*

That's called self-reflection. Now, Callie may not have the answers right away, but this self-reflection is a very important first step toward building her self-awareness. If she does this regularly, she'll soon understand herself better and know why she does what she does, empowering herself to think things over before she has knee-jerk reactions in the future.

When you self-reflect, you explore the hidden layers of yourself that influence your choices and behaviors. It allows you to figure out what's going on inside your mind and heart. It's like being your own investigator, Sherlock Holmes style, but without the fancy hat and magnifying glass.

It's not always easy to self-reflect, though. We live in a crazy, fast-paced world filled with distractions like social media and Netflix. But carving out some quiet time for yourself, away from buzzing phones and binge-worthy shows, is totally worth it because self-reflection is a powerful tool for personal growth. It just helps you to respond better in tough situations.

Like, remember that time you got into a heated argument with your best friend? Well, self-reflection gives you the chance to think before you speak instead of blurting out hurtful words. It can help you make better choices and build healthier relationships.

Next time you find yourself in a sticky situation or feel confused about your emotions, try to self-reflect. It's like peeling back the layers of an onion (minus the tears, hopefully) and discovering the gem you truly are. Take a moment to pause, ask yourself some questions, and dig a little deeper. You might just find the clarity you've been searching for.

The benefits of self-reflection

You get to know yourself

Self-reflection helps you understand your core values, which are like your personal guiding principles. Knowing your values can make life's decisions a lot easier because you'll have a clear idea of what truly matters to you.

Discover your potential

Self-reflection is a powerful way of discovering your special talents and learning about your purpose in life so you can use it to make a positive impact on the world. It also gives you an opportunity to learn more about your strengths and weaknesses, which is pretty important for knowing where you rock and where you can improve.

Self-reflection makes you a big-picture thinker

Instead of getting caught up in the little things, you'll be able to see the grand scheme of things. It's like putting on a pair of special shades that allow you to see beyond the mundane and into the extraordinary. Seeing the big picture puts life in perspective and makes it easier to handle challenges, understand different viewpoints, and make better decisions.

Face your fears head-on

We all have things that scare us, but when you take time to reflect on your fears, you realize they're not as bad as they seem. It's like shining a flashlight on those dark corners and finding out there's nothing to be afraid of. Self-reflection makes you braver and more resilient.

Deeper connections

Self-reflection is great for building people skills. When you know yourself better, you tend to connect with people on a deeper level, have greater empathy, and can elicit a sense of appreciation for who you truly are. That's because most people simply gravitate toward authenticity.

Good vibes and good sleep

Self-reflection can help you keep your cool and handle tough situations without getting anxious or stressed out. Every time you self-reflect, you get a glimpse into what triggers your emotions, and you gain insights into how you can act differently if conflict arises or something potentially stressful happens. Your subconscious takes note of your discoveries and, when the time comes, it guides you to react calmly. And if you do some self-reflection before bedtime, it helps to clear your mind so you can enjoy a great night's rest.

Remember, self-reflection is not about being hard on yourself or getting stuck in a loop of self-criticism. It's about accepting and loving yourself—flaws and all. It's like giving yourself a big bear hug and saying, "Hey, I'm pretty fabulous just the way I am!"

RECAP: UNDERSTANDING SELF-REFLECTION

. . .

Self-reflection is like being your own detective, where you get to explore your thoughts and emotions to understand yourself better. It helps you make better choices, build healthier relationships, and unleash your potential. Above all, self-reflection is about accepting and loving everything that makes you you.

What is mindfulness?

Mindfulness is the ability to enter the ultimate state of chill by letting go and simply enjoying the present moment to the max. It's a moment of bliss where you release yourself from overthinking everything.

Here's the deal: We all tend to zone out and get lost in our own thoughts, right? It's totally normal, however, sometimes it makes us feel anxious and disconnected . . .

What about this thing?

What about that thing?

What if . . . ?

You know how it goes. Luckily, there's mindfulness. It's a super effective way to snap yourself back to reality so you stay cool and collected. You can try all sorts of different ways to practice mindfulness, like chill meditation sessions, taking mindful walks, or even combining it with activities you love, like yoga or sports.

Embracing mindfulness is like saying "peace out" to stress, and it comes with perks:

- You can boost your performance in all areas of life.
- You can become better at cultivating self-awareness and gain even deeper insights about yourself.
- And you can be more attuned to the well-being of your family, friends, and classmates.

But mindfulness isn't just about sitting cross-legged and chanting "om." It's an entire lifestyle. It's about being super aware of everything you do, from brushing your teeth to dealing with your annoying little brother or sister.

Why, you may ask, is mindfulness such a big deal? Let's find out.

The benefits of mindfulness

Stress-busting magic

Mindfulness is like a stress-repellent shield. It helps you feel more relaxed, even when things get intense. You'll learn to handle stress well and boost your overall well-being.

Happiness booster

Feeling down? Mindfulness can help turn that sinking feeling into bliss, like a happiness potion for your brain. Research shows that mindfulness can reduce anxiety and depression, improve your mood, and make you feel calmer and more clear-headed.

It activates your concentration

Do you ever find your mind wandering off like a mischievous cat? Well, mindfulness can tame it by strengthening your focus and attention skills. You'll become the envy of your classmates with your quick thinking (not to mention all the tests you'll ace).

Better emotional regulation

Mindfulness gives you the power to handle your emotions like a pro, leaving you feeling more balanced and in control.

Mind and body fitness

Mindfulness practice can help lower blood pressure, ease consistent pain, improve sleep quality, and even boost your immune system. Plus, mindful eating can help you make healthier food choices and maintain a healthy physique.

Self-discovery

Mindfulness helps you become more aware of yourself, your thoughts, and your feelings. You'll gain a deeper understanding of who you are and learn to love yourself just the way you are. You're amazing, remember that!

Brain flexibility

Mindfulness gives your brain some serious flexibility training, kind of like yoga for your mind. You'll become a master of adaptability, creative problem-solving, and making smart choices.

RECAP: UNDERSTANDING MINDFULNESS

Mindfulness is the ultimate state of chill that helps you stay present and stress-free. It's a skill you can develop through super easy techniques that enhance all areas of your life. A mindful life reduces stress, boosts happiness, improves focus, and enhances emotional control. It benefits your mind and body, fosters self-discovery, supercharges relationships, and trains your brain to be flexible.

Now that you've got the theory of self-awareness down, it's time to get practical. Head over to Chapter 5 to learn some fun techniques.

CHAPTER 5
FOOL-PROOF STRATEGIES FOR CULTIVATING SELF-AWARENESS

> "Of course I talk to myself! Sometimes I need expert advice."

ANONYMOUS

SELF-AWARENESS EXERCISES

Get curious about yourself

Cultivating self-awareness is like embarking on an epic journey of self-exploration. Picture your mind and heart as uncharted territory, just waiting for you to set foot on its unexplored paths.

Before you go to bed every night, take a moment to reflect on your thoughts, feelings, and actions of that day. The idea is to reflect, so don't get caught up in overanalyzing yourself or engaging in negative self-talk. Think of it as having a nonjudgmental conversation with a close friend and asking questions that can unlock the secrets of your inner world. Here are some ideas:

1. What were the highlights of my day? What made me feel happy, proud, or fulfilled?

2. Were there any challenges or setbacks I faced today? How did I handle them, and what can I learn from those experiences?
3. Did I show kindness or help someone today? How did it make me feel?
4. Did I engage in activities or hobbies that brought me joy or relaxation? How did they contribute to my overall well-being?
5. Did I manage my time effectively and prioritize my tasks? Were there any areas where I could improve my productivity?
6. Did I communicate and connect with my friends, family, or peers? Was I positive? Did I listen actively and express myself honestly?
7. Did I take care of my physical health today? Did I eat nutritious food, engage in physical activity, or get enough rest?
8. Did I learn something new today? What knowledge or skills did I gain?
9. Did I practice gratitude today? What am I grateful for in my life right now?
10. What could I have done differently today to make it better? How can I apply these insights to tomorrow?

Remember, self-discovery isn't a one-time event; it's a life-long quest. As you grow and navigate the twists and turns of life, stay curious and keep exploring your passions, strengths, and values. Be open to trying new things and learning from your experiences.

Accept your imperfections

Your flaws and quirks make you a one-of-a-kind and totally interesting person. So, cut yourself some slack. We all mess up sometimes. It's part of being human. Those slip-ups are stepping stones on your path to becoming more self-aware.

Remember that time you tripped over your own feet in front of your crush? Yeah, it was embarrassing, but here's the thing—it's not the end of the world! Instead of beating yourself up over it, try embracing the hilarity of the situation. Laugh it off! Believe me, a good laugh over your own blunders is excellent for your confidence. And hey, your crush might even find your ability to laugh at yourself super attractive.

Whether you're into comic books, love making terrible puns, or have an uncanny talent for mimicking animal sounds, that's what sets you apart from the crowd. Your quirks are the spice that makes life interesting, so own them with pride!

Now, let's talk about those tests that didn't go as planned. Trust me, even your parents have been there, too. It's easy to get down on yourself when you don't ace something you worked hard for. But success isn't linear and it's not about winning all the time. It's also about showing resilience and having true character when things don't go your way.

You know the saying about being a sore loser? Don't be one.

When you make a mistake or don't get the grade you wanted, take a deep breath and figure out what you can learn from the experience, and do it with a smile. Maybe you need to study more effectively, learn to ask for help sometimes, or simply give yourself a break when you're feeling overwhelmed. Embracing imperfection means accepting defeat and being open to improvement at the same time. That's how you discover your own unique strengths.

Take mirror time

This strategy isn't about perfecting your selfie game or practicing your smoldering gaze (although those can be fun, too). Instead, it's a me-time activity of getting to know yourself on a deeper level.

Here's how to do it:

Step 1: Choose a calm and private area where you feel comfortable and can have uninterrupted mirror time. Ensure you have access to a mirror or the front-view camera on your phone (preferably a mirror so your phone's notifications don't distract you!).

Step 2: Set a timer for five minutes and promise yourself you'll stay focused on the activity until the time runs out, and then settle into a relaxed and comfortable position in front of the mirror.

Step 3: Begin by observing the subtle nuances of your facial expressions. Notice the movements of your eyebrows, lips, and eyes. Pay attention to the emotions that arise and flicker across your face. See if you can spot the shifts in your facial features that reflect happiness, sadness, excitement, or other emotions. Stay present and allow yourself to experience and acknowledge these emotions without judgment. Reflect on the patterns you notice in your reactions, facial expressions, and body language. Are there certain triggers that consistently evoke specific emotions? Do you notice any habitual responses or gestures? Consider how these patterns might influence your daily experiences and interactions with others. Next, shift your focus to your body language. Observe how you hold yourself, the tension or relaxation in your muscles, and any gestures you make.

Step 4: When the five minutes are over, reflect on significant insights or realizations that emerged during the activity (better yet, write these reflections somewhere). Consider how this newfound self-awareness can empower you to navigate life and set an intention to carry your newfound self-awareness into your daily life.

Why does this activity matter, you ask?

Mirror time is an opportunity to deepen your connection with yourself. Accept the vulnerability and messiness of being human. Embrace the idea that you are worth your own time, attention, and love. By observing your reactions and emotions, you become more attuned to your inner state. You can recognize patterns and understand what makes you tick. It's like unlocking a treasure trove of self-knowledge.

When you know what triggers certain emotions or how your body language reflects your mood, you become a master of your own destiny. You're no longer at the mercy of random emotions or those knee-jerk reactions and can face life with intention and grace.

Mirror time may sound weird, but it works. The more you connect with yourself, the more you'll understand the reasons behind your behavior, feel empowered to change the things you don't like about yourself, and embrace the beautiful messiness of being human.

Journal your journey

You'd be surprised at what happens when you put pen to paper (or fingers to keyboard). Jotting down your emotions and thoughts can bring so much clarity and insight. It allows you to notice patterns, triggers, and the things that make your heart sing or your blood boil. It's like shining a spotlight on your inner world and saying, "Hey, I see you, emotions, and I'm ready to understand you better!"

Whether you find yourself in a tricky situation or are facing a mental mountain you need to conquer, your journal can be a trusted confidant. Not only does journaling give you a place to pour out your heart, but it serves as your personal time machine. Seriously, when you look back at your previous entries, you'll see just how much you've grown and evolved despite the obstacles.

Journaling isn't just about capturing the tough stuff, though. It's also a place to celebrate the little triumphs, the joyful moments, and the beauty of everyday life. Write about the things that light you up, the dreams you're chasing, and the experiences that make your heart do a happy dance.

Your journal is your sacred space to unravel the mysteries of your mind and heart, so let your thoughts dance across those pages. Explore your inner landscape, discover your strengths, and embrace your vulnerabilities. It's a great tool for self-awareness, growth, and self-acceptance. Above all, remember that journaling is a personal journey. There are no rules or judgments—it's just you and the blank pages waiting to be filled.

Hang out with real people

Personal feedback only goes so far, so spending time with real people in your quest to understand yourself better is pretty important. And, no, digital interactions alone won't cut it.

Spending too much time online can eventually make you feel disconnected from the real world and make you miss out on little but important things happening around you, like the joy of a good hug or the pleasure of a shared joke. Besides, you won't know if there's a secret standup comedian or motivational guru living inside you if you don't mingle face-to-face.

When you engage with others in person, you get to share authentic experiences, have deep conversations, and truly listen to what others have to say. There's something special about being able to see someone's facial expressions, hear the tone of their voice, and feel their energy. It adds a whole extra layer of connection that emojis and GIFs just can't replicate.

When you hang out with people, their feedback can help you gain insights and perspectives about yourself. They can reveal things you might not have discovered on your own. Plus, nothing compares to heartfelt moments with your tribe. Those are the memories you'll cherish and the stories you'll be telling your grandkids someday (or maybe your holographic AI assistant in the future, who knows?).

Step away from the virtual world every once in a while and immerse yourself in the richness of human connection. The magic of real-life connections is something you don't want to miss out on.

MINDFULNESS EXERCISES

Mindful breathing

Find a cozy spot where you can relax with zero interruptions for at least five minutes. Maybe it's your favorite corner in your room or that oh-so-comfy bean bag chair. Now, close your eyes and take a moment to settle in. Focus on your breath—that magical rhythm of life flowing in and out of you. Notice the air as it enters your nostrils, maybe even feel how it tickles your nose hairs.

Breathe in . . . 1 . . . 2 . . . 3.

Let the air fill your lungs, like you're taking in all the good vibes of the universe.

Breathe out . . . 1 . . . 2 . . . 3.

As you exhale, let go of any muscle tension or mental stress. Feel the calmness washing over you like a wave gently caressing the shore.

Keep focusing on your breath.

Inhale and imagine all the positivity and confidence entering your body.

Exhale and let go of any doubts or negativity that might be holding you back.

Mindful breathing gives your brain a super relaxing spa treatment, pampering it with peaceful thoughts and tranquility. You'll notice the stress melting away, leaving you feeling refreshed and grounded.

Remember, mindfulness is all about being fully present in the moment. So, whenever you feel overwhelmed or need a confidence boost, pause what you're doing and take five minutes to tune in to your breath. It's like pressing the reset button and giving yourself the space to recharge and embrace your inner strength.

Even if you're in the middle of something and can't get away, you can use this exercise to calm your nerves right there and then. Trust me, it's that powerful! Focus on your breath with deep inhales and exhales until all your concentration shifts to your breathing, then ease back into the task at hand with renewed focus.

Mindful munching

It's time to take your snacking game to a whole new level. So, grab a tasty treat, whether it's a juicy piece of fruit or a scrumptious health cracker, and let's dive in!

Find a cozy spot in your kitchen (or wherever you feel most comfortable). Before you indulge, take a good look at your snack. Push all the thoughts out of your mind until your only concern is that yummy thing in your hand. Notice its colors, its shape, and how it's calling out to your taste buds.

Bring the snack closer to your nose and inhale deeply. Can you smell that mouthwatering aroma? Let the scents awaken your senses and build up the anticipation. It's like a prelude to the flavor symphony about to unfold!

Finally, take that first glorious bite.

But wait! Don't rush.

Take your time to feel the snack's texture against your lips and tongue. Is it smooth, crunchy, or perhaps a bit of both? As you chew, pay attention to how it feels in your mouth. Is it soft and juicy, or does it have a satisfying crunch? Notice the flavors as they activate your taste buds. Sweet, tangy, savory, or a delightful combination of them all? Let each bite be a moment of pure culinary bliss.

Chew slowly. Feel the food nourishing your body. Be fully present in this moment, free from all distractions. Relish the deliciousness. Immerse yourself in the experience with each bite. Notice how the flavors evolve and how your enjoyment deepens.

Mindful munching is not just about feeding your body. It's about feeding your soul. It's about celebrating the simple pleasures of life, even if it's just a snack in your kitchen. Take a moment to appreciate the experience and nourishment you've given your body. You've just transformed snacking into an art form!

Walk the zen way

Although you'll be moving for this exercise, the workout is more about your mind than your body, so take a slow(ish) stroll for at least 15 minutes and tune in to the present moment. Notice the sensation of the ground beneath your feet, whether it's the softness of grass, the pavement beneath your soles, or the crunch of leaves (you'll get a good sense of it even if you're wearing shoes). Treat each step like a gentle reminder to stay grounded and connected to the here and now.

As you move forward, broaden your senses from the ground beneath you to the world around you. Listen to the symphony of nature—the rustle of leaves in the breeze, the chirping of birds, or the distant hum of traffic. Let these sounds become the soundtrack of your journey, but don't let your thoughts wander—just focus on the sights, smells, and sounds around you. Notice the intricate details of the vibrant colors of flowers, the patterns on the bark of trees, graffiti on walls, or the way sunlight dances on and through various surfaces. It's like discovering a whole new universe right in your neighborhood!

Enjoy each moment of your walk with complete awareness. Feel the gentle breeze on your skin, savor the fresh air filling your lungs, and take in the scents of nature. Let it awaken your senses and remind you of the beauty that surrounds you. And hey, keep those eyes peeled for any unexpected surprises. Who knows, you might spot a squirrel doing a funky dance or a butterfly gracefully fluttering by.

Walking can be so much more than getting from point A to point B. It's a chance to embrace the world around you, be fully present in each step, and discover the beauty in ordinary things. As you reach the end of your walk, take a moment to appreciate the tranquility and sense of peace you've cultivated in so little time.

Puzzle time

Engaging in puzzles is not only a fun pastime but also an excellent mindful workout for your brain. Whether it's a word search, Sudoku, a brain teaser, or an old-fashioned jigsaw puzzle, they require focus, attention to detail, and problem-solving skills. By immersing yourself in the puzzle-solving process, you can experience a heightened state of concentration and mental clarity.

Appreciate the intricacies of each clue or puzzle piece. Notice how your mind becomes sharp and focused as you analyze the information and consider possible solutions. You know that feeling when you're fully immersed in something and everything just clicks? That's called the state of flow. It's super satisfying and easy to achieve when doing puzzles.

Sometimes, it can be difficult to immerse yourself in a puzzle from the get-go because of distracting thoughts. If that happens, sit back, and do the mindful breathing exercise. Once you're solely focused on your breathing, switch over to the puzzle and let all that focused energy flow into solving it.

Puzzle time is also the perfect opportunity to challenge yourself in a controlled and enjoyable manner. Each puzzle presents a unique set of problems to solve, and with each solved clue or completed puzzle, you experience a sense of accomplishment. This feeling of success and mastery can boost your confidence and self-esteem, reinforcing the belief in your abilities to overcome challenges. Beyond the immediate enjoyment and sense of accomplishment, engaging in puzzle time regularly can have long-term benefits for your cognitive abilities. By consistently exercising those cognitive skills, you can improve your mental agility, creativity, and critical thinking abilities.

Tech detox dance party

Technology has a nasty way of taking over every aspect of life. How many times have you grabbed your phone to record something epic instead of just absorbing the moment? It's not an accusation—I can't even keep track of how many times I've done it. And when I'm not careful, I find myself glued to my phone or tablet while hundreds of posts compete for my already divided attention.

The tech detox dance party offers a refreshing break from technology overload and an opportunity to let go and just enjoy the moment.

Dancing is a form of self-expression and a powerful way to connect with your body and emotions. As you surrender to the music, you release pent-up stress and tension. The physicality of dancing stimulates the release of endorphins (your natural happy hormones) and promotes a sense of ultimate well-being. It's like a burst of positive energy surging through your veins that releases you from the worries and stresses of life so you can reconnect with joy and playfulness. As you crank up the tunes, let the rhythm guide your movements. Dance like nobody's watching (because they're not, you know?).

This is your moment to let go of self-consciousness and fully enjoy yourself. Move freely and forget about judgments and expectations. Feel the music pulsating through your body as it ignites your energy and sets your spirit free.

END-OF-CHAPTER ACTIVITY: JUST DO IT, 'CAUSE THERE'S NO TIME LIKE NOW

Choose any technique from this chapter to do right now.

Before you start, grab a notepad and pen, and answer the following questions:

1. What is my current level of stress or anxiety on a scale of 1 to 10?

2. How would I describe my overall mood and emotional state right now?

3. How am I feeling physically?

4. How present am I at this moment? Am I fully aware of my surroundings?

5. What is one intention or goal I have for this practice? What do I hope to gain or experience?

When you're done, answer the following questions:

1. What is my current level of stress or anxiety on a scale of 1 to 10 compared to before the exercise?

2. How would I describe my overall mood and emotional state now? Has it shifted in any way?

3. How does my body feel now?

4. How present and aware was I during the exercise? Did my mind wander frequently, or was I able to maintain focus?

5. Did the exercise meet my expectations or intentions? In what ways did it positively impact me?

That's it—you're now a self-awareness guru in your own right!

But remember, self-awareness doesn't just happen. Like any relationship with a friend, you'll have to spend quality time with yourself if you want it to work, so come back to the exercises in this chapter often.

Don't forget, if you ever need a refresher on the ins and outs of self-awareness, flip back to the *Recap* section of this chapter.

Now it's time to expand your confidence into the exciting realm of positive self-talk.

Ready? See you in Chapter 6.

CHAPTER 6
CULTIVATING POSITIVE SELF-TALK LIKE A BOSS

> *"Self-talk reflects your innermost feelings."*

DR. ASA DON BROWN

WHAT IS POSITIVE SELF-TALK?

Self-talk is like having a little commentator inside your head, chatting away all day long. It's your internal dialogue, consisting of a mix of your thoughts, beliefs, questions, and ideas. The way you talk to yourself is a powerful force that can impact how you feel and what you do.

When self-talk is positive, it's like having your own cheerleader or team of supporters, motivating you and boosting your confidence. Thinking positively about yourself results in you feeling oh-so-good and optimistic. It improves your self-esteem, helps you manage stress, and makes you more resilient in the face of challenges. When self-talk turns nasty, though, it becomes an annoying little voice that brings you down and makes you doubt yourself. This is called negative self-talk, and it's a real buzzkill. It's like a cloud of doubt that doesn't reflect reality but still makes you feel like you're going to fail even before you start.

The most important thing to know about self-talk is that you *always* have the power to make that voice more positive and supportive. We'll dive much deeper into this topic in the rest of the chapter, but for now, here are some cool tips that will help you conquer negative self-talk:

- Practice self-awareness.
- Recognize those negative thoughts the moment they appear and question if they're true or just exaggerations.
- Put things into perspective. Ask yourself if what you're worrying about will even matter in a few days, weeks, months, or years.
- Stop the thought. Visualize a stop sign or have your own little ritual to interrupt those negative thoughts. No one's watching!
- Replace the thought. Swap that negativity with kindness and encouragement.

Changing self-talk is like building a new habit; it takes time and effort. But you've got this, and together with the other techniques you've already learned, it will be your ultimate confidence-boosting weapon to rock at life!

RECAP: WHAT IS POSITIVE SELF-TALK?

It's all about being your own biggest fan with internal words of praise, motivation, and encouragement. And, yes, you can totally talk to yourself out loud. Adults do it all the time!

BEWARE OF NEGATIVE SELF-TALK

Josh was the school's best storyteller—hands-down. Everyone believed he had a bright future that involved becoming a famous author or screenwriter. While he knew he had talent and appreci-ated everyone's enthusiasm, Josh had a dark companion that never left his side . . . his inner critic.

Every time he sat down to write, that inner critic would rear its ugly head and bombard him with endless negativity.

"You're not good enough," it would say, *"your writing is terrible, no one will ever read it."*

These thoughts took root in Josh's mind, and he began to doubt his abilities and question whether pursuing his dream of writing was worth it. Sadly, Josh never learned to challenge his negative self-talk. He let it consume him, and eventually, he stopped writing altogether. He never shared his stories with anyone, and the world never got to experience the magic of his words. His fear of failure and lack of confidence in his abilities kept him stuck in a cycle of self-doubt and inaction. Over time, Josh's passion for storytelling dwindled, and he settled for a more conventional career path that felt safer—but it left him unfulfilled. He looked back on his school days and wondered what could have been if he had only found the courage to ignore his inner critic and pursue his dream.

Negative self-talk doesn't just get you down the moment it happens. As you can see from Josh's story, it comes with serious consequences if you fail to take control and turn it into positive self-talk. Let's have a closer look at what these consequences are.

Lack of confidence

You can follow every strategy in this book to build your confi-dence, but if you talk yourself down all the time, they'll mean nothing. That's because when negative self-talk takes over, you can't see your true potential anymore. Self-doubt will reign in your mind and your confidence will remain very low. Imagine feeling like you're not good enough all the time. No fun, right? It's *that* important to kick negative self-talk to the curb.

Decreased motivation and feeling helpless

Negative self-talk can drain your motivation like a leaky bucket. This lack of motivation will soon leave you feeling out of control and like you have no direction whatsoever. We call that feeling helplessness, and it can mess with your entire life on so many levels.

Increased anxiety and heightened stress

Negative self-talk can leave you feeling like you're carrying a heavy burden every day. It can also create problems out of thin air, leading to more stress and anxiety. Your mind will play tricks on you and make you believe almost any worst-case scenario it imagines. This constant worry and anxiety can be overwhelming and exhausting, and the worst part (or best part—depending on your point of view!) is that most worries never, ever come true.

> *"Ninety-eight percent of the things we worry about never happen."*
>
> DALE CARNEGIE, *HOW TO STOP WORRYING AND START LIVING*

It can silence your voice and send you into hiding

You are destined for greatness. Your thoughts and ideas matter. But you can jinx yourself into the abyss of mediocrity if you give in to negative self-talk. It can force you to dim your light and hide your true self from the world. The truth is, you have so much to give, and your thoughts and opinions deserve to be heard—it's the only way you can make the world a better place. Don't allow negative thoughts to keep you from sharing your awesomeness with others!

Predictability and boredom

When you default to negative thoughts, your MO is to play it safe and stay in your comfort zone. It's like being stuck in a bubble where everything is predictable. Sure, predictability feels safe, but it's also boring. Life is meant to be exciting and full of adventures, and you deserve to experience all the amazing things it has to offer.

Limited thinking and missed opportunities

Negative self-talk clouds your vision and puts limits on what you believe you can achieve. It's like building invisible walls around your potential that prevent you from seeing the possibilities right in front of you. Opportunities often present themselves disguised as challenges, and you want to be able to recognize them. You can't do that if you're busy dissing yourself all the time. Remember that your thoughts shape your reality, so you owe it to yourself to create a supportive and positive internal dialogue.

Relationship issues and lack of connection with others

Speaking of walls, negative self-talk can make you put them up around your heart and avoid being vulnerable with others. It can also make you feel insecure and needy in close relationships. Meaningful relationships thrive on openness and trust, and as a social being, you really do need people if you're going to live life to the fullest.

Some serious regrets at the end of your life

Imagine this: You've lived your life and now you're old. Looking back, all you can see are missed opportunities, dreams left unfulfilled, and adventures never taken. Ouch.

As a teen, you have your whole life ahead of you, and it's filled with countless possibilities and opportunities. Don't entertain negative self-talk. If you do, it will convince you that you're incapable of achieving success and leave you feeling like you don't deserve happiness. You'll find yourself looking back with endless regret, wondering what could have been.

RECAP: NEGATIVE SELF-TALK IS A TOTAL KILLJOY

It saps your confidence, kills motivation, and fuels anxiety. It silences your voice, limits your thinking, and can leave you with regrets. Don't let it hold you back from living your best life and pursuing your dreams . . . Kick negative self-talk to the curb and embrace a positive, empowered mindset. You've got this!

Phew! With all that negativity out of the way, let's see what you have to gain from the opposite of the coin.

THE BENEFITS OF POSITIVE SELF-TALK

Let's see how Josh's life could have turned out if he had learned to beat his negative self-talk.

Maybe his dad realized what was happening and took it upon himself to help Josh.

As he watched his son struggle, Josh's dad didn't want him to experience the same regrets and unfulfilled dreams he had faced in his own life. He knew the answer was for Josh to challenge his negative self-talk. So, he decided to become Josh's mentor and biggest cheerleader. He encouraged him to share his stories with him and the rest of the family. Whenever the young writer faced self-doubt, his dad was there to remind him of his incredible talent and the positive impact his stories made.

Together, they learned techniques to challenge negative thoughts. They gave Josh's inner critic a funny nickname—Mr. Gloomy Grouch—and turned it into a playful game to disarm its power. Josh's dad reassured him constantly that negative self-talk was normal but conquerable.

With his dad's support and guidance, Josh began to see his writing in a new light. He realized that he was genuinely capable of pursuing his dreams. Every time the negative self-talk crept in, Josh turned it into positivity that motivated him to push through. His confidence grew and his writing flourished.

Years later, as Josh stood on a stage, accepting an award for his bestselling novel, he couldn't help but feel grateful for his dad's intervention. He knew that without it, he might have succumbed to his inner critic and never pursued his writing dreams. But he also knew that if he wasn't a fighter who could learn to believe in himself, his dad's efforts wouldn't have worked.

See how life can turn out radically different depending on how you talk to yourself? The question is, what kind of life do *you* want to live?

It doesn't matter what challenges get thrown your way, you always have the choice to (1) let it defeat you, or (2) let it be an invitation for growth and success. Which one you choose will depend a lot on your mindset, and your mindset depends on how you talk to yourself.

Let's explore some benefits you can gain from cultivating positive self-talk.

Improved self-esteem

You're truly amazing and engaging in positive self-talk will ensure you never forget it. When you fill your mind with encouraging words and thoughts, your self-esteem gets a mega boost. You'll walk with your head held high, knowing that you're a superstar in your own right. So, take a good look at yourself in the mirror and embrace thoughts like "You're capable" and "You're worthy."

Healthier immune system and increased vitality

Positive thoughts encourage your body to release happy chemicals that boost your immune system, kind of like a secret health-boosting potion. This means your body will be on alert and ready to fight whenever bugs try to invade and mess with you.

Positive self-talk also works its magic in your body's energy department. It pumps you full of life and vitality so you can make the most of every moment.

Less Pain

Who knew thoughts could have a say in how much something hurts? It's true! Positive self-talk is like a soothing balm for your brain. It sends calming signals to your nervous system, telling it to turn down the pain volume. When you have to face a needle at the doctor's office or deal with a sore muscle after a workout, remember to be kind to yourself. Say things like "You're strong; you can totally handle this," and watch how it eases the ache.

Your heart will thank you

When you think positively, your heart feels lighter and happier, just like when you hear your favorite jam. A happy heart is a healthy heart. By keeping yourself busy with uplifting thoughts instead of negative ones, you're helping your heart to stay in tip-top shape.

A strong mind

By now, you've learned that life can be a wild ride. Positive self-talk is like a safety harness that protects your mental health on really bad days. When you talk kindly to yourself, you build resilience. Think of it as a mental muscle that helps you to stay confident and ready to bounce back from tough times.

Less stress

You know those negative thoughts that try to make you worry and freak out that we talked about earlier? They've got nothing on your positive self-talk shield. Positive thoughts will always help you see a way out, and even if things go wrong, you'll know it's not the end of the world. Besides, when you're more focused on how well you're handling life, there's really no time for worrying.

Killer coping skills

Engaging in positive self-talk doesn't mean trying to ignore the fact that life can be hard to deal with. Setbacks will happen (a lot), but positive self-talk is the umbrella that keeps you dry in the storm. It helps you find the strength to handle tough times, learn from them, and grow into a strong person and a role model of resilience to others.

Better relationships and stronger connections with others

Positive self-talk helps you build a strong foundation of self-love and kindness. When you treat yourself with respect, that good energy radiates to others, too. You're more open to forming connections and this allows you to become a better friend, sibling, or boyfriend/girlfriend because you know how to uplift and support others.

Superhuman focus

Got a goal in mind? Positive self-talk helps you lock onto that target like a laser beam. When your thoughts are positive and clear, distractions don't stand a chance. You're in the zone like a video game character focused on winning. You'll stay on track and crush your goals like a pro gamer taking down the final boss.

No regrets and greater life satisfaction

Life is like a colorful canvas, and positive self-talk is the paint-brush that adds the vibrant strokes of happiness. When you embrace positivity, you see life through a kaleidoscope of bright possibilities. You're more grateful for the little things and find joy in the simplest of moments. And you're not afraid to step out of your comfort zone, which means you can live life the way you were meant to. With a positive outlook, you'll create a masterpiece of a life characterized by satisfaction and contentment. And, as a bonus, there's a chance that you'll live a little longer than your grumpy neighbors. Studies show that optimistic people tend to live longer because they don't stress too much when life throws curveballs at them.

RECAP: POSITIVE SELF-TALK TO THE RESCUE!

Positive self-talk is like a forcefield that protects your mind and body. It boosts self-esteem, strengthens your immune system, and eases pain. Your heart dances with joy, and you become a mental powerhouse, able to conquer challenges with resilience. It builds better relationships and laser-like focus in everything you do. Embrace positivity for a vibrant, regret-free life full of satisfaction and true happiness.

REWRITING NEGATIVE SELF-TALK WITH POSITIVE AFFIRMATIONS

First off, it's important to know that you can't completely stop your thoughts. Every person's mind is busy, so it's always chatty. That's totally normal. While you can't stop your thoughts, you can definitely change how you talk to yourself. That's why some people look so miserable, and others look like they're about to indulge in the best ice cream ever—like every day.

Overcoming negative self-talk starts with self-awareness. You can only catch those thoughts in the act if you're aware of what's happening in your mind. With all the knowledge you've gained about self-awareness from the previous chapters, you've already laid a strong foundation for overcoming any negativity that may be haunting you. The next big step is to challenge your negative thoughts—another skill you've already learned in the previous chapters. All you need to do now is practice and build on it, and you'll do that with a powerful mental tool called affirmations.

What are affirmations?

They're simply statements you say to yourself repeatedly. Affirmations can be negative ("You're so stupid!") or positive ("You're brilliant and it's OK to make mistakes."). To rewrite negative self-talk, you should turn your negative affirmations into positive affirmations. It's simple. It's powerful. And it can boost your confidence, self-esteem, and overall well-being. Think of positive affirmations as little pep talks you give yourself to create a positive and empowering mindset.

It may sound fluffy and perhaps a little awkward, but these guys are solidly backed by science. There's an entire branch of psychology dedicated to it, called self-affirmation theory.

It doesn't end there, though.

Neuroscientists were interested in finding out if affirmations have an effect on the brain's physiology, and it turns out they do! They've discovered that practicing positive affirmations increases specific neural pathways in the brain. So, yeah, positive affirmations really do work.

But there's a catch: They only work if you practice them regularly.

RECAP: THERE'S MAGIC IN AFFIRMATIONS

Or . . . There's science in affirmations (which is kind of the same thing!). You have the power to change how you think and feel about yourself by simply making positive statements about yourself. These statements are known as positive affirmations, and the key to success is regular practice.

Twenty positive affirmations you can start using right now

The best affirmations are the ones you come up with by yourself, for yourself, because you're unique and you have your own brand of love and light to share with the world. At the end of the chapter, I'll guide you on a fun activity to do just that. But since crafting your own positive affirmations can take some time, start by practicing any of the below statements in the meantime. Pick at least five that resonate with you the most, write them down, and start using them every day from this moment onward.

By the way, there's an interesting debate in the self-development community about whether affirmations are more effective when you state them in the first person (as in "I'm a math genius") or second person (as in "You're a math genius"). So, I'll leave the verdict up to you. Try your affirmations both ways and then self-reflect on which version really makes an impact on how you feel.

1. *I'm confident. I believe in my abilities and can achieve whatever I want.*
2. *I am loved and people care about me.*
3. *I'm not perfect, and that's OK because I'm good enough just the way I am.*
4. *I love my quirks and flaws. They make me unique.*
5. *I'm worthy of love and respect, even when I make mistakes.*
6. *My opinions matter and I have a right to speak up.*
7. *I don't have to be strong all the time—I'm allowed to feel angry or disappointed or scared.*
8. *I don't have to have all the answers to feel good about myself.*
9. *I'm grateful for what I have and I'm a generous person.*
10. *I value and respect other people just as much as I value and respect myself.*
11. *I have self-respect and don't have to compromise my morals for anyone.*

12. *I don't compare myself to others because we're all unique and special in our own right.*
13. *I'm an important part of my family.*
14. *I'm important to my friends.*
15. *I'm focused and fully capable of reaching my goals.*
16. *I love receiving help from other people when I can't figure things out on my own.*
17. *I'm courageous and can stand up for myself.*
18. *I love life, no matter what challenges it throws my way.*
19. *I am dependable.*
20. *I am a reliable friend all the time.*

END-OF-CHAPTER ACTIVITY: CREATE YOUR OWN AFFIRMATIONS

Step 1: Identify a negative thought.
Think about thoughts that have been holding you back or making you feel insecure. It could be that pesky voice saying, "I'm not good enough" or "I'll never succeed."

Step 2: Turn it into a positive affirmation.
Now, let's turn that negative thought upside down! Write down the positive opposite that counters your belief. For example, if you feel like "I'm not smart enough," change it to "I am intelligent and capable."

Step 3: Keep it short and sweet.
Short affirmations are super effective and easy to remember. You can even make it fun and catchy! For example, "I'm bold and unstoppable."

Step 4: Add emotion and make it present.
Make your affirmation come alive. Add some feeling to it by saying things like "I am excited about my potential" or "I feel confident in myself."
Also, affirmations work best in the present tense, so be sure to use "I am" or "You are" statements.

Step 5: Repeat, repeat, repeat!
Repetition is the key to the success of positive affirmations, so commit to saying yours daily. You can write them on sticky notes and put them all over your room and in strategic places like your mirror for a daily reminder.

Step 6: Stay real and believe in yourself.
Make sure your affirmations feel real and achievable to you. If a certain affirmation feels too far-fetched, scrap it, or soften it with "I am open to the idea of . . ." or "I am willing to believe I can . . ."

Step 7: Bonus tip . . . Get inspired!
If you need some inspiration, check out lists of premade affirmations that suit your goals. You can find ideas online or in self-help books.

Always remember that self-talk is a powerful tool. It can shape your mindset and transform your life for the better or for the worse—which way it goes is totally up to you.

Life is so much better when it's filled with positive self-talk, so dump the negativity, embrace the magic of affirmations, and pave the way for a vibrant and fulfilling life. You've got the power to be your own biggest fan and achieve greatness—go for it!

Next, we'll tackle a biggie: dealing with social pressure. See you in Chapter 7.

CHAPTER 7
BEYOND THE CROWD – OVERCOMING SOCIAL PRESSURE

> *"Be yourself because an original is worth more than just a copy."*

SUZY KASSEM

WHAT IS SOCIAL PRESSURE?

So, you totally get that you're unique, and you really want to embrace that idea. It's a pretty big deal because, honestly, what's so special about being like everyone else? Yet there's this thing that's always urging you to do anything to fit in . . . You can't see it, you can't touch it, and you can't really describe it—but you can *feel* it.

It lingers in the air every time you're in class or hanging with your friends or doing something in public with your family. It makes you self-conscious, forces you to make sure you're dressed right, that your hair looks OK, or that you're saying the appropriate words and using the right tone of voice and lingo—even if it doesn't sound remotely like the regular you.

That feeling is called social pressure, and it's the beast of all confidence killers.

Social pressure is like an invisible force that pushes you to conform to other people's expectations against your will. And it's super easy to give in because if you don't, you risk disappointing people, being judged harshly, and even being made fun of and labeled as some coward or the spoilsport in the crowd.

It's a tough challenge that leaves you in a classical catch-22 situation: If you don't give in to social pressure, you get to stay true to yourself, but you might be left standing all alone. And if you go with the flow just to fit in, you betray your true self but at least you've got a spot in the crowd and people like you.

None of those sound like they can leave you feeling confident, do they?

Is social pressure your friend or foe?

The thing is; social pressure isn't black and white. There are gray areas, and if you know how to navigate them, your confidence will not only remain intact, but it will also flourish.

So, no, social pressure isn't all bad.

In fact, it's quite useful in giving you the bump you need to move outside of your comfort zone in some cases.

Take Ben . . . He's a good friend because he's always available to support his pals. They like spending time with him because, despite needing motivation like 99% of the time, he's actually a great sport. Ben isn't a big risk taker and is left to his own devices; he'd be home reading or playing video games every free second of his life.

But that's where social pressure saves the day.

His friends normally invite him on action-filled adventures like mountain biking and rock climbing. He always says no, and then they tease him about it. Most of the time, Ben gives in and goes along. On the rare occasion that he doesn't go along, his friends let the issue go, too, and they never judge or treat him differently when he sits out. But when Ben goes on the adventures, he actually ends up having immense fun. Lately, he's even been contemplating taking up mountain biking as a sport.

In Ben's case, the social pressure he's under is good for him, because it allows him to explore life outside of his comfort zone (reading and video games) and gives him the opportunity to discover more about himself. And, as it turns out, he enjoys the activities with his friends so much that he wants to take it further. Who knows, maybe he'll become a world champ in mountain biking or some other adrenaline-fueled sport. The fact is, if it weren't for social pressure, Ben would probably never have discovered this hidden passion.

On the other hand, social pressure has a dark side.

Remember Aubrey, your friend who wants to travel, but his dad wants him to go to law school? Let's say Aubrey is so afraid of disappointing his dad that he ignores what *he* wants to do and applies for law school.

He pushes through, but he's miserable. In time, he retreats into himself even more and doesn't even talk to you about the things he was once so passionate about. Now, if he told you he had discovered that becoming a lawyer is fantastic and that it turns out he's passionate about it just like his dad, that would be fine.

But he hates it.

And you can see it in his face and hear it in his voice . . . He's living someone else's life.

In Aubrey's case, bending under social pressure has resulted in a personal disaster for him. If he doesn't build the confidence to get himself out of that trap soon, his life can turn out pretty terrible.

There's an important point to make here, though, and that's the fact that Aubrey never talked with his dad about how he really feels. Aubrey just knows that his dad has this vision for him, and he believes that if he doesn't fulfill that vision, his dad will be disappointed and reject him. Mostly, though, parents just want their kids to be happy. They may have different ideas about what that "happy" should look like, but that doesn't mean they won't accept a different version.

You owe it to yourself and your parents to be open with them about your plans and dreams. And if you're honestly terrified of telling them, maybe try the '*Beat fear and anxiety before they beat you*' exercise at the end of Chapter 3 before having a chat with them. If that doesn't help, there's nothing wrong with confiding in a trusted teacher or another adult you look up to. They'll help you get through it in the best way possible.

RECAP: UNDER PRESSURE . . .

Social pressure is that incredibly strong urge you feel to conform to people's expectations and to fit in—no matter what. Depending on the nature of the social pressure, it can be good or bad for you. When it comes to family expectations, your best strategy is to be true to yourself and be very honest about your interests and passions with your parents.

How to know the difference between helpful social pressure and toxic social pressure

It's super important to realize that social pressure is not only an important part of your life right now, but something that will be a part of it pretty much forever. You can never avoid it, but you can manage and beat it. That's how you can stay confident and always stay true to yourself, no matter what.

A big part of navigating social pressure involves knowing when it can serve you and when it can sink you. Let's see how helpful social pressure differs from toxic social pressure.

What to look out for	Helpful social pressure	Toxic social pressure
Alignment with Personal Values	Encourages you to try new experiences, explore your interests, and step outside of your comfort zone while still aligning with your core values and beliefs.	Pushes you to act in ways that go against your values, beliefs, or ethical standards, causing internal conflict and discomfort.
Positive Growth vs. Negative Consequences	Leads to positive personal growth, self-discovery, and expanded horizons. It helps you discover hidden talents and passions, like in the case of Ben, who found a new interest in mountain biking.	Results in negative consequences for your mental, emotional, or physical well-being, like Aubrey, who experienced misery and lost touch with his true passions.
Respectful Boundaries	Respects your boundaries and allows you to say no without fear of judgment or ridicule. Your friends and peers understand and accept your choices, even if they differ from theirs.	Disregards your boundaries and insists on compliance without considering your feelings or preferences. It may involve manipulation, ridicule, or emotional blackmail to get you to conform.
Empowerment vs. Helplessness	Empowers you to make informed decisions for yourself, promoting independence and self-confidence.	Makes you feel helpless or trapped, as if you have no choice but to conform to others' expectations, leading to a loss of self-esteem.
Long-Term vs. Short-Term Impact	Positively impacts your life in the long run.	Provides short-term relief by fitting in momentarily, but it can have lasting negative effects on your self-esteem and emotional well-being.
Supportive vs. Destructive	Comes from friends or peers who genuinely care about your well-being and support your growth and happiness.	Originates from individuals or groups who seek to control or manipulate you for their benefit, often at the expense of your happiness and authenticity.
Open Communication	Encourages open communication and understanding among friends, allowing for honest discussions about differences and choices.	Thrives on secrecy and fear, discouraging open communication and authentic expression of thoughts and feelings.

WHERE DOES SOCIAL PRESSURE COME FROM?

Peer pressure

This is a big one when it comes to social pressure, and you've probably heard the term many times. It's when people (mostly your friends or peers your age) use all sorts of tactics to get you involved in activities. You may be reluctant to participate because you're not interested, or you've got a little fear of the unknown, or the idea may simply clash with your values and give you bad vibes.

Sometimes, peer pressure can motivate you to do better in school or try new things (like Ben), which can be excellent for your morale and confidence. But, watch out, because it can also be tricky when it leads you to take risks or do things that don't match with your true self (like Aubrey).

Repeat after me: Fitting in and pleasing others is *never* a good reason to buckle under peer pressure. If you do something, do it because you *want* to.

> *"To live is to choose. But to choose well, you must know who you are and what you stand for, where you want to go and why you want to get there."*
>
> KOFI ANNAN

An intense need to belong

As you grow up, friends become super important in your life. You want to belong and be accepted by your social circle, right? Nothing wrong with that.

Maybe you look up to your friends and feel the pressure to be like them. This is why self-reflection is so crucial. It can bring up questions like *"Why do I want to be like them so badly?"* If the answer is superficial, something along the lines of wanting to be cool like them or "just because," those aren't good reasons. Have you thought about the possibility that maybe they want to be more like you? Or that the reason they hang out with you is because they like you just the way you are? Being yourself is by far the coolest thing you can do! You already belong, and you're doing just fine.

Now, if your friends want you to change and will reject you if you don't, they're not really your friends, are they? *They* don't belong with *you*. You have every right to be yourself in all your glory, just like them.

Most of the time, though, friends aren't that nasty. Mostly, the fear that you don't belong is a lie from none other than your pesky self-doubt gremlin. You already know how to handle that guy (check back to Chapter 2 if you need a recap).

On the flip side, you may feel the need to be more like a friend who's disciplined and focused on their goals, or maybe they have a way of cruising through challenges with optimism. Those are fantastic qualities, so if you feel inspired to be more like your friend in that regard, go for it. But the trick is to cultivate the same qualities your friend has, *not* to copy their personality. It's like seeing something that resonates with you and thinking, "I should try that but with my own twist!"

Family and cultural expectations

Your family and cultural background also have a stake in the social pressure pie. The values, traditions, and family expectations you grew up with can greatly influence the choices you make. That's perfectly fine if they resonate with you, but sometimes, this pressure can push you to make decisions only because you feel obligated to conform to get a stamp of approval.

This kind of pressure is probably the toughest to overcome, because going your own way has the potential of creating a rift between you and the people you love the most, especially if your family values their legacy and traditions above everything else.

The best advice in this regard is this: First, remember that you're the one who has to live with your choices for the rest of your life— not your family. Second, never underestimate the power of communication. If you can be crystal clear about your interests, passions, and expectations from life, your family will very likely want to see you excel in that—even if they don't agree or understand.

School

This ties in with cultural and family pressure because it has a lot to do with what you believe people expect of you. The drive to do well in classes, sports, or extracurricular activities can put a big load of pressure on your shoulders.

To take some of that load off, review your sports and extracurricular activities. Are you doing them because you love it or need it for your future, or because you think it's expected of you? If you're doing things that aren't enriching your existence or securing your future, just stop!

Seriously, life is too short to please other people at the expense of your own peace and happiness.

If you're doing everything you love and you still feel overwhelmed, an easy fix is to prioritize and schedule. You'll be amazed at the free time that appears out of thin air when you practice a little discipline in your daily life.

Social media

Remember comparisonitis from Chapter 2? Social media is the biggest source of social pressure that exists today. In addition to fighting the urge to compare yourself with the online versions of your friends and peers, you have to deal with endless ads about what's hot and not.

Don't be fooled.

The people who create ads and targeted posts are psychology buffs who know how to get inside your head and make your self-doubt gremlin take notice. Challenge what you see in the same way you challenge your negative thoughts. Are they true? Does your life really depend on going with that flow? Or is it a plot to suck the uniqueness out of you?

Remember, if you do what everybody else is doing, you might just as well be a soulless robot. Social media gives all of us a skewed perception of life. Go out there, mingle, and you'll soon see that most people don't even remotely represent all the stuff you see online.

RECAP: SOURCES OF SOCIAL PRESSURE

Social pressure can come at you from every angle, but the biggest one you should be aware of is social media. Other sources are your need to fit in, peer pressure, school, and expectations from your family.

THE CONNECTION BETWEEN SOCIAL PRESSURE AND YOUR MENTAL HEALTH

At your age, you're especially vulnerable to the effects of social pressure on your mental health because you're still discovering the real you—the authentic person you want to become one day. If you can't manage social pressure and resist it when necessary, it can make you feel like someone's playing yo-yo with your mind and identity. You'll soon feel lost and disconnected from yourself, and that can open the doors to stress, anxiety, and even depression.

In 2019, a British investigative program revealed that a whopping 68% of young people (aged 16 to 30) thought they could have mental health issues. But that's not the worst part. Apparently, many teens have gotten so used to feeling down that they might not even realize they're experiencing anxiety and depression symptoms, and 37% of young people don't feel confident. On the other hand, there has been so much hype around mental health issues that a staggering number of teens believe they have anxiety and depression when, in reality, they're just experiencing the motions of growing up. Many studies over the years have proven that there's a definite correlation between social pressure and mental health issues, especially for young people.

Point in case: Your sanity totally depends on your ability to overcome social pressure.

A PEEK INTO THE EFFECTS OF SOCIAL PRESSURE

Emotional overload

At the end of the day, we're social creatures, and we just want to love and be loved. But the pressure that comes with that desire can cause some intense emotions.

Sometimes, it can feel like you're constantly on edge, trying to keep up with what (you think) others want or think of you.

But here's a secret: Your mind is pretty resilient, and despite all the noise out there about mental health problems, it's not going to let you down that easily, especially if you nourish it with everything you've been learning in these pages. Take care of your precious mind, and I promise, it will take care of you.

A drowning self-esteem

This is that thing I talked about earlier about feeling disconnected from yourself. The influence of social pressure can make you think you have to mold your personality, interests, and beliefs to fit in. In serious cases, it can cause an identity crisis, where you're unsure of who you really are or what you genuinely value.

It's not a fun place to be in, so remind yourself every day that it's not only OK to embrace yourself and your unique qualities, but also a requirement for a confident life.

Struggles with your body image

Social pressure often revolves around appearance and body image and—you guessed it—social media dictates the pace here. Never, ever fall for those unrealistic beauty standards and expectations.

You're beautiful, handsome, gorgeous, and smokin' hot just the way you are. You tick all the right boxes, so go ahead and fall in love with what you see in the mirror! If you *want* to change anything, like maybe getting fitter or a little stronger, do it for the right reasons. Otherwise, move on, 'cause there's not one inch of yourself to be ashamed of.

Increased temptation to take part in risky behavior

Peer pressure can be a strong toxic motivator for engaging in things you'd normally not even think of. You might feel the pull to try substances, engage in dangerous stunts, or break rules just to fit in. Don't fall into this ditch. It doesn't have a bottom and the people who pushed you in won't hang around to throw you a life-line. They're not your friends. Always use your critical thinking cap and consider the consequences of risky temptations very, very carefully.

Academic issues

The pressure to perform academically can have the opposite effect of what you hope or expect; it can eventually lead to burnout and bad grades. Then there's the whole juggling act between trying to maintain good grades, being superb in those extracurriculars, and being a decent friend. The key here is to find a way to balance all of it. Try different strategies and schedules until you find something that makes you feel more in control and chill.

Feeling isolated

Want to know what's weird? The harder you try to fit in, the more alone and uncertain you feel. It makes you stressed and anxious about being rejected or judged, and to avoid that, you simply withdraw and keep to yourself. Genuine and meaningful connections come from being yourself and finding people who appreciate you for who you are.

RECAP: HOW SOCIAL PRESSURE AFFECTS YOUR LIFE

From emotional distress to feeling tempted to do risky stuff, social pressure can make you feel like you're being pushed into a corner with no way out. There's a clear link between your mental health and experiencing social pressure, and if you can't fight it, life can get pretty depressing.

But that's not the end of the story, because you CAN fight back.

HOW TO OVERCOME SOCIAL PRESSURE

Meet your ultimate weapon: assertiveness

You know how sometimes you're too shy to speak up, and then later you're like "Ugh, why didn't I just say something!?" Or maybe you've seen someone who was way too pushy and in-your-face while talking to another someone, and your inner voice was like "Whoa . . . Take it down a notch!"

None of those are helpful in social interactions . . . You want to strike a balance between being a total pushover and being rude. That's where assertiveness comes in. Being assertive means you can express your thoughts, feelings, and needs in an honest and respectful way. You don't have to be afraid to share your ideas, ask for what you want, or disagree with someone. It's about knowing your worth and believing that your ideas matter as much as anyone else's. But at the same time, it's also about being open and respectful, and mindful of other people's opinions and feelings.

Assertiveness is a skill you can learn with some willpower and practice, so no worries if you're on the shy side. You've come a really long way since Chapter 1, and with all the skills you've gained so far, assertiveness will be second nature for you in no time.

The benefits of being assertive

You can help cultivate better understanding between yourself and other people

Don't you just hate it when someone doesn't get what you're saying? And then they turn around to tell you that you're the one who doesn't get them . . . It's so annoying, I know.

The real issue isn't comprehension. It's a lack of communication. For some reason, we tend to think other people are supposed to know what's going on in our heads. We talk to ourselves all the time, so we totally get ourselves, but when those words come out, they're not exactly articulate.

But when you're assertive, you don't assume the person you're talking to knows what you're thinking, so you make a point of expressing yourself well. And that makes you a great help, too, because it encourages them to do the same. Then, like magic, the two of you understand each other perfectly.

Less drama

Miscommunication is the biggest reason people bicker and fight. And then, as if we assume the other person has a hearing problem, we raise our voices to get the point across. But no matter how loud we go, they just don't get it . . .

Assertiveness comes with a level of tact you'll learn to appreciate; there's no need to yell, like ever. You'll be able to share your point of view calmly, respectfully, and crystal clear. It's by far the most effective way to prevent misunderstandings from turning into total blowouts. Conflict is stressful, and you don't need it in your life.

Getting your needs met

I bet you've felt the sting of having your needs overlooked or ignored. It really hurts. And it sucks. The thing is, it probably wasn't done on purpose. These things happen when people don't really know what you need. When you learn to be assertive, people are more likely to listen and respond positively. It's like opening the door to getting what you deserve and making sure your voice is heard.

Now that you've got the theory down, it's time to get practical and add assertiveness to your confidence-boosting toolbox so you can overcome social pressure.

RECAP: ASSERTIVENESS HAS THE LAST SAY

Assertiveness is the ultimate weapon against social pressure. It's a communication method that allows you to say exactly what you need, want, and expect—all while being a nice person who respects others.

How to be an assertive communicator

Make eye contact

When you're talking with someone, try to look them in the eye. It shows that you're confident and really engaged in the conversation. But don't stare them down like you're in a staring contest or anything—just keep it natural.

Use a strong but nonaggressive tone of voice

Your tone can change how your message comes across. So, when you're standing up for yourself or expressing your thoughts, use a firm tone that shows you mean business, but don't sound angry or pushy.

Be like "Hey, I've got something to say," not like "You better listen to me right now!"

Be mindful of your facial expressions

Your face can say a lot without you even realizing it. So, pay attention to your expressions. If you're trying to be assertive, keep a calm and composed face. Smiling is fine, but don't grin like you just heard a joke in the middle of a serious conversation.

Let your timing be perfect

You want to wait for the right moment to say something, even if it's very important. Don't try to nudge it into a busy or stressful situation, and make sure the other person isn't in a hurry. That way, they can give you their full attention. Also, when you're in the middle of the conversation, don't interrupt the other person. Listen and only reply when they're done.

Be specific

Always be clear when you're expressing yourself. Avoid vague language that can lead to misunderstandings and make sure the words coming out of your mouth are actually saying what you mean.

Be nonthreatening

Being assertive doesn't mean acting in an aggressive or scary way. Don't give off angry vibes, don't invade the other person's personal bubble, and stay away from threatening language. Just chill and be respectful.

Frame your messages positively

Use sensitive and constructive language and focus on keeping yourself cool and calm. Use words that show you want to find a solution or work things out. Be in control of your emotions. If the other person has some negative feedback, don't feel offended. Ask them to tell you more so you can deal with the issue objectively.

Use "I" statements

"I" statements keep the conversation personal, honest, and nonjudgmental. For instance, saying something like "I feel this way," or "I think we can do this," sounds much better than just throwing blame on the other person.

Be an active listener

Listening is just as important as talking. Give the other person your full attention. Show you care by nodding or making little noises to let them know you're following along.

Value yourself and your rights

Remember, you're wonderful, and you deserve to be treated with respect. Stand up for yourself and your rights, and don't let anyone walk all over you (but be decent about it).

Stay calm even if the other person overreacts or gives off negative vibes

Sometimes people can get all worked up, but that doesn't mean you have to join in on the drama. Your calmness can help diffuse tense situations.

Accept criticism and praise

Everyone has their ups and downs, and it's cool to take criticism and praise with an open mind because you can learn from both. Don't get hung up on criticism if you receive it—it's just another opportunity to grow and become better.

END-OF-CHAPTER ACTIVITY: GRAB A FRIEND AND HONE YOUR ASSERTIVENESS

Step 1: Find a partner.
First things first, find a friend who's down to improve their assertiveness with you. It can be someone you're close to, like your best friend, or someone you're comfortable with but haven't hung out with in a while. The important thing is that you both agree to support each other.

Step 2: Brainstorm assertiveness scenarios.
Now, brainstorm different scenarios where assertive communication would come in handy. These could be

everyday situations, like deciding on what movie to watch, or more serious ones, like expressing your opinions in a group setting.

Step 3: Role-play.
Time to put on your acting hats! Review all the assertiveness techniques we discussed above and then take turns role-playing the scenarios you came up with. One of you will play the assertive communicator, while the other takes on the role of the other person in the situation.
Remember, this is just for practice, so feel free to have fun with it.
Switch roles every now and then.

Step 4: Give and receive feedback.
After each role-play, take a minute or two to give each other constructive feedback. Chat about what went well and what could be improved.

Step 5: Reflect and set goals.
When you're done practicing, take a moment to reflect on what you've learned. Discuss how it felt to practice assertive communication and what you both took away from the experience. Based on your reflections, set some personal goals for how you can be more assertive in your daily lives.

READY TO CHANGE SOMEONE'S LIFE?

Let's fulfill my promise to the man in the park with a bang! With your help, I can reach even more people, and he'll have had more of an impact than he'll ever know.

Simply by sharing your honest opinion of this book and a little about your own journey, you'll show other young people where to go to start their own story of improved confidence.

In under one minute, you can help others just like yourself by leaving a review! Thank you so much for your support. You're making more of a difference than you realize.

CONCLUSION

Confidence is the armor that shields you from doubt, the fuel that propels you forward, no matter what, and the light that guides your path.

High five to you for sticking around and exploring the world of confidence and self-discovery!

I hope you've found valuable insights and inspiration and that you're walking away with a new-found, unshakable confidence. Above all, I hope you'll embrace yourself from now on—all of you —because the world is such a better place with your uniqueness.

Throughout these pages, we've explored the importance of confidence as the key to navigating life's challenges and opportunities. You now know it's not a gift anyone is born with; it's a skill that can be cultivated through deliberate practice and an unwavering belief in your abilities. The power to shape your future is entirely in your hands, no matter your background or circumstances.

I shared my own experiences, as well as those of other teens, to offer you relatable perspectives and a guiding light. But now it's your turn. Embrace the journey ahead and whatever happens, stay true to yourself. The road may get bumpy and twisty, but I know you've got the right mindset to handle it like it's no one's business. You're strong and you can handle anything life throws at you. And remember, setbacks are the best opportunities to learn and grow.

As you navigate this exciting, weird, and wonderful ride called life, know that you're never alone. Seek support from friends, family, mentors, or even a kind stranger on a park bench (unless they look dodgy). Wherever you go, there will always be someone who believes in you and wants to see you thrive.

Your teenage years are a one-of-a-kind and a once-in-a-lifetime rite of passage, a perfect time to build a solid foundation for the future. Embrace the challenges, embrace yourself, and most importantly, have fun! Time has a way of flying by without you even noticing, so don't waste a second trying to please others or fitting in where you're not appreciated.

Remember, confidence is not about perfection; it's about accepting and believing in yourself—flaws, quirks, and all the rest.

REFERENCES

CHAPTER 1 REFERENCES

Abdou, A. (2021, August 5). The 2 types of confidence, according to science (and how to harness them). *Ladders | Business News & Career Advice*. https://www. theladders.com/career-advice/the-2-types-of-confidence-according-to-science-and-how-to-harness-them

Admin. (2021). Why is confidence so important? *MindBodySpirit Festival*. https://www.mbsfestival.com.au/healthy-living-hub/confidence-importance/

Confidence (for Teens) - Nemours KidsHealth. (n.d.). https://kidshealth.org/en/teens/confidence.html

Cullum, T. (2018, May 6). What is Social Confidence Anyway? - Todd Cullum - Medium. *Medium*. https://medium.com/@ToddCullum/what-is-social-confidence-anyway-8ca8f669d785

Eikenberry, K. (2012). The Confidence/Competence Loop. *The Kevin Eikenberry Group*. https://kevineikenberry.com/leadership/the-confidencecompetence-loop/

Espinosa, C. (2021). How The Confidence Competence Loop Can Benefit You. *Christian Espinosa*. https://christianespinosa.com/blog/how-the-confidence-competence-loop-can-benefit-you/

Happiful Magazine. (n.d.). Is Neuroscience the Key to Confidence? *Happiful Magazine*. https://happiful.com/is-neuroscience-the-key-to-confidence

Inc.Africa. (n.d.). https://incafrica.com/article/minda-zetlin-confidence-social-epistemic-julia-galef-how-to-build-confidence

Inc.Africa. (n.d.). https://incafrica.com/library/geoffrey-james-if-youve-got-this-1-character-trait-youll-probably-be-successful-according-to-neuroscience

Jenkins, P. (2023, July 4). Why Confidence Is Important (and How to Boost It) - Brilliantio. *Brilliantio*. https://brilliantio.com/why-confidence-is-important/

LinkedIn. (n.d.). https://www.linkedin.com/pulse/how-neuroscience-can-make-you-more-confident-malhotra-acc-cpcc/

The confidence – competence loop. (n.d.). https://www.carolynecrowe.co.uk/blog/the-confidence-competence-loop/

Today, P. (2023, June 26). Confidence. Psychology Today. https://www.psychologytoday.com/us/basics/confidence

Van Leeuwen, N. (2022). Two Concepts of Belief Strength: Epistemic Confidence and Identity Centrality. *Frontiers in Psychology*, *13*. https://doi.org/10.3389/fpsyg.2022.939949

Wall, A. (2020, September 8). What Confidence is and is Not, and How to Get More of it in Your Life. *Athena*. https://www.athenastemwomen.org/post/what-confidence-is-and-is-not-and-how-to-get-more-of-it-in-your-life

What Confidence Is and Is Not - by Joyce Shafer. (n.d.). https://trans4mind.com/counterpoint/index-happiness-wellbeing/shafer17.html

CHAPTER 2 REFERENCES

Beresin, E., MD. (2022, June 3). Low Self-Esteem in Adolescents: What Are the Root Causes? Psychology Today. https://www.psychologytoday.com/intl/blog/inside-out-outside-in/202206/low-self-esteem-in-adolescents-what-are-the-root-causes

Bergagna, E., & Tartaglia, S. (2018). Self-esteem, social comparison, and Facebook use. *Europe's Journal of Psychology, 14*(4), 831–845. https://doi.org/10.5964/ejop.v14i4.1592

Chong, J. (2023). Low self-esteem: The role of social comparison — The Skill Collective. *The Skill Collective*. https://theskillcollective.com/blog/low-self-esteem-social-comparison

MSEd, K. C. (2022). Social Comparison Theory in Psychology. *Verywell Mind*. https://www.verywellmind.com/what-is-the-social-comparison-process-2795872

Self-Confidence Starts Early. (n.d.). Urban Child Institute. http://www.urbanchildinstitute.org/articles/features/self-confidence-starts-early

Self-esteem and teenagers - ReachOut Parents. (n.d.). https://parents.au.reachout.com/common-concerns/everyday-issues/self-esteem-and-teenagers

Sharma, I. (2021, April 16). Does Confidence Issues Stem From Your Childhood? - Blog - HealthifyMe. *HealthifyMe*. https://www.healthifyme.com/blog/does-confidence-issues-stem-from-your-childhood/

Shawi, A. F. A., & Lafta, R. (2015). Relation between childhood experiences and adults' self-esteem: A sample from Baghdad. *Qatar Medical Journal, 2014*(2). https://doi.org/10.5339/qmj.2014.14

Sma-Admin. (2022, April 11). *3 Causes of Low Self-Esteem in Teens (And What to Do About It) - Stop Medicine Abuse*. Stop Medicine Abuse. https://stopmedicineabuse.org/blog/details/3-causes-of-low-self-esteem-in-teens-and-what-to-do-about-it/

CHAPTER 3 REFERENCES

Account, S. (2022). 3 Things Your Teens Fear the Most. *Focus on the Family*. https://www.focusonthefamily.com/parenting/3-things-your-teens-fear-the-most/

Anxiety (for Teens) - Nemours KidsHealth. (n.d.). https://kidshealth.org/en/teens/anxiety.html

Department of Health & Human Services. (n.d.). *Trauma and teenagers – common reactions*. Better Health Channel. https://www.betterhealth.vic.gov.au/health/healthyliving/trauma-and-teenagers-common-reactions

REFERENCES

Miller, C., Bubrick, J., PhD, & Anderson, D., PhD. (2023). How Anxiety Affects Teenagers. *Child Mind Institute.* https://childmind.org/article/signs-of-anxiety-in-teenagers/

mindbodygreen. (2022, September 21). *10 Signs Fear Is Running Your Life (And How To Get Back On Track).* Mindbodygreen. https://www.mindbodygreen.com/articles/signs-fear-is-running-your-life

Pickhardt, C. E., PhD. (2013, November 11). Appreciating Fear in Adolescence. *Psychology Today.* https://www.psychologytoday.com/us/blog/surviving-your-childs-adolescence/201311/appreciating-fear-in-adolescence

Stieg, C. (2020, March 20). How fear influences your behavior, and how to cope. *CNBC.* https://www.cnbc.com/2020/03/20/how-fear-influences-your-behavior-and-how-to-cope.html

SupaduDev. (2023). 4 Fear-Based Routines That Get You Stuck. *New Harbinger Publications, Inc.* https://www.newharbinger.com/blog/self-help/4-fear-based-routines-that-get-you-stuck/

Tosh, D. (2023). How to Recognize That Fear is Driving Your Behaviour — Phoenix-Hearted Woman. *Phoenix-Hearted Woman.* https://www.phoenixheartedwoman.com/blog/how-to-recognize-that-fear-is-driving-your-behaviour

CHAPTER 4 REFERENCES

Bailey, J. R. (2022, March 21). *Don't Underestimate the Power of Self-Reflection.* Harvard Business Review. https://hbr.org/2022/03/dont-underestimate-the-power-of-self-reflection

Botelho, G. (2020, November 30). Building Self-Confidence Through Self-Awareness I HR Exchange Network. *HR Exchange Network.* https://www.hrexchangenetwork.com/employee-engagement/columns/building-self-confidence-through-self-awareness

Capp, K. M. B. (2023). Top 11 Benefits of Self-Awareness According to Science. *PositivePsychology.com.* https://positivepsychology.com/benefits-of-self-awareness/

Davenport, B. (2022). The Benefits Of Practicing Self-Reflection. *Mindful Zen.* https://mindfulzen.co/benefits-self-reflection/

Davis, D. M., & Hayes, J. A. (n.d.). What are the benefits of mindfulness. *https://www.apa.org.* https://www.apa.org/monitor/2012/07-08/ce-corner

Dowches-Wheeler, J. (2021). How Self-Awareness Builds Confidence — Bright Space Coaching I Leadership Development for Women. *Bright Space Coaching I Leadership Development for Women.* https://www.brightspacecoaching.com/blog/2018/6/20/how-self-awareness-builds-confidence

Eurich, T. (2023, April 6). *What Self-Awareness Really Is (and How to Cultivate It).* Harvard Business Review. https://hbr.org/2018/01/what-self-awareness-really-is-and-how-to-cultivate-it

Habash, C. (2022). What is self-reflection? Why is self-reflection important? *Thrive-*

works. https://thriveworks.com/blog/importance-self-reflection-improvement/

Humber River Health. (2022, January 27). *The Benefits of Self-Awareness - Humber River Health.* https://www.hrh.ca/2022/01/27/the-benefits-of-self-awareness/

Jennifer. (2023, March 2). 10 Benefits of Self Awareness And How it Can Impact Your Life –. . . *Contentment Questing.* https://contentmentquesting.com/benefits-of-self-awareness/

LinkedIn. (n.d.). https://www.linkedin.com/pulse/link-between-confidence-self-awareness-grant-henderson/

Mindfulness Definition | What Is Mindfulness. (n.d.). Greater Good. https://greatergood.berkeley.edu/topic/mindfulness/definition

Mindfulness for Your Health. (2022, July 15). NIH News in Health. https://newsinhealth.nih.gov/2021/06/mindfulness-your-health

MSEd, K. C. (2023). What Is Self-Awareness? *Verywell Mind. https://www.verywellmind.com/what-is-self-awareness-2795023*

Self Awareness & Confidence. (n.d.). https://www.ulster.ac.uk/employability/advice/digital-learning-hub/self-awareness-and-confidence

Self-Reflection 101: What is self-reflection? Why is reflection important? And how to reflect. | Reflection.app — Your guided journal for wellness and growth. (n.d.). https://www.reflection.app/blog/self-reflection-101-what-is-self-reflection-why-is-reflection-important

Self Reflection - Benefits, Importance, and How To Do It | Toggl Track. (n.d.). https://toggl.com/track/self-reflection/

Self-Reflection: Definition and How to Do It. (n.d.). The Berkeley Well-Being Institute. https://www.berkeleywellbeing.com/what-is-self-reflection.html

Smith, M., MA. (2023). Benefits of Mindfulness. *HelpGuide.org.* https://www.helpguide.org/harvard/benefits-of-mindfulness.htm

Staff, M. (2023). What is Mindfulness? *Mindful.* https://www.mindful.org/what-is-mindfulness/

What Is Self-Awareness, and Why Is It Important? (n.d.). https://www.betterup.com/blog/what-is-self-awareness

What Is Mindfulness? | Taking Charge of Your Health & Wellbeing. (n.d.). Taking Charge of Your Health & Wellbeing. https://www.takingcharge.csh.umn.edu/what-mindfulness

CHAPTER 5 REFERENCES

Capp, K. M. B. (2023). How to Increase Self-Awareness: 16 Activities & Tools (+PDF). *PositivePsychology.com.* https://positivepsychology.com/building-self-awareness-activities/

Choosing Therapy. (2023). Mindfulness for Teens: How It Works, Benefits, & 11 Exercises to Try. *Choosing Therapy.* https://www.choosingtherapy.com/mindfulness-for-teens/

REFERENCES

How the power of storytelling can change the course of your career. (2019, November 6). [Video]. NBC News. https://www.nbcnews.com/better/lifestyle/what-self-awareness-how-can-you-cultivate-it-ncna1067721

Hughes, J. (2022). How to Cultivate Self-Awareness (And Why That's Important). *Elegant Themes Blog.* https://www.elegantthemes.com/blog/business/how-to-cultivate-self-awareness

Mindfulness Exercises (for Teens) - Nemours KidsHealth. (n.d.). https://kidshealth.org/en/teens/mindful-exercises.html

Our Top Mindfulness Activities For Teens. (2021, February 7). Tutor Doctor. https://www.tutordoctor.co.uk/blog/2021/february/our-top-mindfulness-activities-for-teens/

Tjan, A. K. (2015, February 11). *5 Ways to Become More Self-Aware.* Harvard Business Review. https://hbr.org/2015/02/5-ways-to-become-more-self-aware

CHAPTER 6 REFERENCES

Admin. (2020). 4 Benefits of Positive Affirmations. *HeadWay Clinic.* https://www.headwayclinic.ca/4-benefits-positive-affirmations/

Affirmations: What Are They and How Do They Work? (n.d.). https://www.familycentre.org/news/post/affirmations-what-are-they-and-how-do-they-work

Beau, A. (n.d.). How to Spot and Swap the 4 Types of Negative Self-Talk. *Shine.* https://advice.theshineapp.com/articles/how-to-spot-and-swap-the-4-types-of-negative-self-talk/

Footprints To Recovery Addiction Treatment Centers. (2021). *7 Ways to Combat Negative Self-Talk. Footprints to Recovery | Drug Rehab & Alcohol Addiction Treatment Centers.* https://footprintstorecovery.com/blog/combat-negative-self-talk/

Healthdirect Australia. (n.d.). *Self-talk. What Is It and Why Is It Important? |* Healthdirect. https://www.healthdirect.gov.au/self-talk

Helfand, E. (2022). The Benefits of Positive Affirmations. *Wellspring Center for Prevention.* https://wellspringprevention.org/blog/the-benefits-of-positive-affirmations/

Holland, K. (2020, June 27). *Positive Self-Talk: How Talking to Yourself Is a Good Thing.* Healthline. https://www.healthline.com/health/positive-self-talk

How To Stop Negative Self-Talk - Headspace. (n.d.). Headspace. https://www.headspace.com/mindfulness/stop-negative-self-talk

Identifying Negative Automatic Thought Patterns. (n.d.). Stress & Development Lab. https://sdlab.fas.harvard.edu/cognitive-reappraisal/identifying-negative-automatic-thought-patterns

Inc.Africa. (n.d.). https://incafrica.com/library/yoram-solomon-3-things-you-should-stop-doing-to-turn-on-your-creative-brain

Goldman, R. (2022, November 4). *Affirmations: What They Are and How to Use Them.* EverydayHealth.com. https://www.everydayhealth.com/emotional-health/

what-are-affirmations/

Kristenson, S. (2022). How to Stop Negative Self-Talk: A 14-Step Guide. *Happier Human.* https://www.happierhuman.com/stop-negative-self-talk/

Moore, C. M. P. (2023). Positive Daily Affirmations: Is There Science Behind It? *PositivePsychology.com.* https://positivepsychology.com/daily-affirmations/

Monteleone, D. (n.d.). *Negative Self Talk - What is it and why does it matter?* | *Proactive Health & Movement.* Proactive Health & Movement. https://www.proactivehm.com.au/negative-self-talk-what-is-it-and-why-does-it-matter/

Morris, S. Y. (2016, December 19). *What Are the Benefits of Self-Talk?* Healthline. https://www.healthline.com/health/mental-health/self-talk

Richards, L. (2022, March 18). *What is positive self-talk?* https://www.medicalnewstoday.com/articles/positive-self-talk

Richard. (2022). Affirmations. *Clinical Hypnotherapy Cardiff.* https://www.clinicalhypnotherapy-cardiff.co.uk/affirmations/

Santos, J. (2021). 10 Positive Affirmations for Teens and Young Adults (Free Printables). *But First, Joy.* https://butfirstjoy.com/positive-affirmations-for-teens-young-adults/

Scott, E., PhD. (2022). The Toxic Effects of Negative Self-Talk. *Verywell Mind.* https://www.verywellmind.com/negative-self-talk-and-how-it-affects-us-4161304

Scott, S. (2023). 67 Positive Affirmations for Teens & Young Students. *Happier Human.* https://www.happierhuman.com/positive-affirmations-teens/

Self-Talk. (2020, December 9) *Psychology Today.* https://www.psychologytoday.com/intl/basics/self-talk

The Power of Positive Self Talk (and How You Can Use It). (n.d.). https://www.betterup.com/blog/self-talk

T, M. (2017). 8 Dangers of Negative Self-Talk. *Makeda Pennycooke.* https://makedapennycooke.com/8-dangers-negative-self-talk/

Wignall, N. (2022). 10 Types of Negative Self-Talk (and How to Correct Them). *Nick Wignall.* https://nickwignall.com/negative-self-talk/

CHAPTER 7 REFERENCES

Anxiety on the Rise: Are Societal Pressures to Blame? (2016, August 23) *Destination Hope - Your Destination for Recovery.* https://destinationhope.com/anxiety-rise-societal-pressures-blame/

Hazlegreaves, S. (2019). Social pressure is damaging the mental health of millennials. *Open Access Government.* https://www.openaccessgovernment.org/social-pressure-mental-health-of-millennials/70437/

Lautieri, A. (2019). Social Pressures Influence Mood And Behavior. *MentalHelp.net.* https://www.mentalhelp.net/adolescent-development/social-pressures-mood-and-behavior/

REFERENCES

Peer Pressure (for Teens) - Nemours KidsHealth. (n.d.). https://kidshealth.org/en/teens/peer-pressure.html

Peer pressure or influence: pre-teens and teenagers. (2021, November 3). Raising Children Network. https://raisingchildren.net.au/teens/behaviour/peers-friends-trends/peer-influence

Scripps Health. (2023, April 7). How Does Peer Pressure Affect a Teen's Social Development? *Scripps Health.* https://www.scripps.org/news_items/4648-how-does-peer-pressure-affect-a-teen-s-social-development

Teens and Peer Pressure - Children's Health. (n.d.). https://www.childrens.com/health-wellness/helping-teens-deal-with-peer-pressure

Wpa. (n.d.). Social Anxiety, Social Media and your Mental Health. *WPA.* https://www.wpa.org.uk/health- wellbeing/articles/social-anxiety

REVIEW PAGE REFERENCES

Liles, M. (2022, October 10). *Parade.com.* parade.com. https://parade.com/989608/marynliles/confidence-quotes/

THE SOCIAL TEEN

MASTER CONVERSATION SKILLS, SQUASH SHYNESS, CREATE LASTING FRIENDSHIPS, AND THRIVE IN SOCIAL SITUATIONS

Copyright © 2024 by Marnie David

All rights reserved.

No part of this book may be reproduced in any form or by any electronic or mechanical means, including information storage and retrieval systems, without written permission from the author, except for the use of brief quotations in a book review.

Disclaimer

Although the publisher and the author have made every effort to ensure that the information in this book was correct at press time and while this publication is designed to provide accurate information in regard to the subject matter covered, the publisher and the author assume no responsibility for errors, inaccuracies, omissions, or any other inconsistencies herein and hereby disclaim any liability to any party for any loss, damage, or disruption caused by errors or omissions, whether such errors or omissions result from negligence, accident, or any other cause.

The publisher and the author make no guarantees concerning the level of success you may experience by following the advice and strategies contained in this book, and you accept the risk that results will differ for each individual. The testimonials and examples provided in this book show exceptional results, which may not apply to the average reader, and are not intended to represent or guarantee that you will achieve the same or similar results.

THE CONFIDENT TEEN

Download our FREE Social Anxiety Rescue Pack for teens. Get 100 practical tips to boost confidence, improve conversations, foster friendships, navigate tough talks, and enhance self-awareness. Start your journey today!

INTRODUCTION

Picture this: It's the first day of class at a new high school. You're standing at the entrance, clutching your backpack straps tightly, trying to muster the courage to step through the bustling hallways.

Your heart is pounding so loudly you can hear it in your ears. The clamor of the school feels like a wave crashing over you, yet you feel utterly alone. You scan the crowds, hoping for a familiar face, but everyone seems to be in their own world. The laughter and chatter around you sound distant, and you can't help but feel like you're on the outside looking in.

You finally take a deep breath and walk in, but with every step, your mind races with worries. "*What if no one talks to me? What if I say something stupid?*" These thoughts swirl in your head, creating a storm of anxiety. You find a spot at the back of the classroom, hoping to blend into the walls. As the teacher begins the roll call, you rehearse your name in your head, praying you don't stutter.

This isn't just a case of first-day jitters; this is what it's like to live with social anxiety. For millions of teenagers, scenarios like this are a daily reality, a challenge they face in silence. If you find yourself grappling with situations like these on the daily, know that you're not alone. This book is here for you, offering support and understanding to navigate and face those challenges confidently.

Life As a Teen with Social Anxiety

Let's face it: being a teen isn't a walk in the park. It's more like a walk in a maze where every turn can feel like a new challenge. Dealing with social anxiety as a teen adds *another* layer to this challenge. And it's so much more than just getting butterflies before a presentation; it's as if you're constantly wearing these what-if glasses, and all you can see are the worst-case scenarios. I have been there, and I know *exactly* how you feel.

You want to chat with someone, but your brain hits the brakes with a "*What if they don't like me?*" You think of joining a group, and there's that voice again: "*What if I act awkward or start blushing?*" It's exhausting, right? And it's not only about fear; it's about feeling like you're always on the outside, looking in and trying to understand the secret handshake that everyone else seems to know.

Trying to make friends? It's like trying to ride a bike with a missing pedal. You see others effortlessly cruising through social interactions, and you can't help but wonder, "*How do they make it seem so easy?*" It's as if there's this invisible wall between you and the rest of the world; no matter how much you pedal, you can't seem to break through.

That's the everyday struggle for teens grappling with social anxiety. It's not *just a phase* or something you can shake off with a pep talk. It's a real challenge, but the good news is that it's not the end of the story — not by a long shot.

Stats You Should Know

Let's throw some real talk numbers into the mix. Did you know that about 15 million adults in the United States have social anxiety? And most of them first felt those jitters in their teen years. Think about it: that's like the entire population of Los Angeles and New York City combined, all dealing with social anxiety — mind-blowing, right?

And it's not just about feeling shy or nervous. According to some brainy folks who do lots of research, 70% of teens say anxiety and depression are major issues among their peers. That's more than two-thirds of the teenage population acknowledging that mental health is a big deal.

Now, let's talk about our phones. Sure, they're great for TikTok and keeping up with friends, but 50% of teens feel addicted to their smartphones — ironic, isn't it? These gadgets that are designed to connect us can sometimes make us feel more isolated than ever.

If you think you're fighting these battles solo, these stats are here to tell you that you have a whole army of people in the same boat. That's why finding ways to deal with these challenges matters so much.

What Brought You Here?

So, why did you pick up this book? It might be that you're tired of feeling like a background character in your life story. Perhaps you're a parent watching your kid struggle to make friends and wishing you could do something about it. It could be that one day, you just woke up and thought, "*Enough is enough. I want to join the conversations, not just overhear them.*" Or maybe you're just curious about how to level up your social game.

Whatever the reason for reading this book, something clicked in your brain. That moment when you thought, "*I have got to change this,*" brought you here. You're looking for a real-deal playbook on navigating the wild world of teen social life, and guess what? Your search ends right here.

The SOCIAL Formula

This book is your personal toolbox for dealing with all the social curveballs life throws at you. The SOCIAL formula is an acronym we'll go through chapter by chapter to help you hone in on these skills. Let's take a look at how it's broken down:

- **S**elf-awareness is about getting to know yourself, your strengths, quirks, and areas for personal growth.
- **O**vercoming obstacles is how you will deal with barriers such as shyness or feeling inadequate.
- **C**rafting confident conversations is the art of starting and maintaining conversations, leaving people impressed with your skills.
- **I**nitiating conversations involves taking the first step of overcoming your fears to introduce yourself to others.
- **A**ssembling authentic friendships will lead to real, lasting connections.
- **L**everaging life skills helps you adapt and thrive in any social scenario.

Alright, let's talk about perks. By diving into this book, you're signing up for some incredible benefits. First off, you'll gain self-confidence. We're talking about a major boost in how you see yourself. You'll walk into rooms with a new swagger, ready to mingle like a pro.

Want to improve your conversation game? Who doesn't want that? You'll become a conversational wizard, knowing what to say and how to say it. No awkward silences on your watch!

Building authentic friendships is a biggie on our journey. This step isn't just about making acquaintances; it's about forming those ride-or-die friendships—the kind of friendships where you share memes at 2 AM and have each other's backs.

Are you facing social challenges? You'll learn how to tackle them like a boss. Whether you disagree with a friend or feel out of place at a party, you'll have the tools to deal with it.

And let's not forget personal growth and self-discovery. You'll get to know yourself on a whole new level: your quirks, best features, and everything in between.

Finally, you'll learn to master social situations. You'll get through group projects, get-togethers with friends, and family gatherings — and actually enjoy them.

So, get ready to turn those pages and turn up your social life!

Real-Life Case Studies

Let me start by telling you about Maya. She went from "Can't even say hi in the hallway" to "Class president with a fantastic friend group." She says the SOCIAL method was her secret sauce. Then there's Leo, who used these strategies to finally join the soccer team and make a bunch of new friends. He swears he couldn't have done it without this book. And let's not forget Emma, who overcame her fear of speaking up in class; she's acing presentations and debates like a champ. These teens are making real changes using the power of the SOCIAL method.

Imagine walking into any room and feeling like you own it. You've got this magnetic vibe, drawing people in. You're nailing conversations, making genuine connections left and right — that's the transformation awaiting you. Picture yourself no longer on the sidelines; instead, you are in the heart of every social circle with friendships real and deep. You're not just getting through social situations; you're shining in them, radiating confidence. This isn't just about surviving high school; it's about thriving in life. That's the kind of change we're talking about — a total social makeover, inside and out.

My Story

I decided to write this book because I have been in your shoes and intimately understand your struggle. When I was a teen, social situations were my worst nightmare. I was the one who'd find any excuse to avoid speaking up in class or being in a large group. My heart would race and palms would sweat in almost every social setting. I would accidentally interrupt others during conversations, blush when the spotlight was on me, and mentally play back the blooper reel of every conversation after it was over. It was exhausting and debilitating. But I didn't stay stuck; I pushed through, learned a ton, and came out the other side no longer awkward but a *recovering* awkward person.

I have spent years understanding what works and what doesn't work in the realm of social skills. As a teacher for nearly 20 years, I have worked with hundreds of students, talked to experts, and, most importantly, experimented on myself with these strategies. I transformed from a wallflower into someone who loves the challenge of social interactions.

I call it a challenge because everyday social interactions can still be a hurdle. I still get embarrassed and blush sometimes when I'm around groups of people. I still play back social interactions in my mind and worry if I said the wrong thing.

However, when I notice this happening, I pull out my toolbox of skills to help me get through these difficult situations. I look at it like tackling a challenging video game level. I talk back to that negative voice in my head, and each time I conquer another social interaction, it's a confidence win.

Today, I exude more confidence and self-assurance than ever before. And I'm here to share all that hard-earned wisdom with you. Trust me, if I could get through it, you totally can too.

Why Read This Book?

Before getting your hands on this book, navigating social waters probably felt like trying to assemble a puzzle without the picture on the box. You might have seen others effortlessly making friends, wondering why it wasn't that simple for you. Maybe you have tried a few things, such as mimicking popular kids or keeping to yourself; unfortunately, nothing really clicked for you. It's like being lost in a city without a map. Without clear strategies and understanding, overcoming social hurdles can seem like an endless game of guesswork, leaving you stuck on the sidelines and watching life happen to everyone else.

Why is this book the game-changer you have been looking for? Because it's not just another generic guide with fluffy advice; it's a real, down-to-earth playbook tailored just for you. Whether you're feeling lost in the social maze or just looking to level up your friend-making skills, this book speaks directly to your needs. It's packed with strategies that others like you and I have tried and tested — and they work.

This book understands your aspirations, whether it's about fitting in, standing out, or simply feeling comfortable in your skin. *The Social Teen* is about transforming how you interact with others and how you see yourself. It's about breaking free from the chains of social anxiety, building genuine connections, and crafting a social life that you're excited to wake up to. If you're ready to make a change, then trust me. You're holding the right book in your hands.

See you in Chapter 1!

CHAPTER 1
START WITH SELF-AWARENESS (S)

> "Be yourself; everyone else is already taken." – Oscar Wilde

My Quest to Fit In

In the bustling halls of high school, the struggle to fit in was real. I mean, I get it. As a teenager, I was right there in the thick of it, trying to balance the desire to be part of the cool crowd with the fear of standing out like a sore thumb. It felt like walking a tightrope, you know?

I vividly remember a particular Friday night. I was hanging out with my friends at a get-together; the energy was high, and the atmosphere was filled with laughter and camaraderie. But as the night went on, I realized that I was putting on an act. I was laughing at jokes I didn't find funny and nodding with opinions I disagreed with. Then it hit me like a ton of bricks – I was pretending to be someone else just to fit in. This was not me.

In the following weeks, I couldn't shake this weird feeling of emptiness. I lost sight of who I was in my quest to fit in. After lots of self-reflection, I knew what I had to do. I needed to break free from this cookie-cutter version of myself and get in touch with the real me.

So, I started doing things I genuinely enjoyed, speaking my mind even if it went against the grain and letting my unique personality shine through. Let me tell you, it wasn't always smooth sailing. Stepping away from my cozy conformity zone was uncomfortable at times. But here's the kicker: something unique began to happen.

As I embraced my authenticity, my circle of friends changed naturally. I began to form real, genuine connections. During my teen years, I learned that real friendships are created when you are true to yourself. When you let your authentic self shine, you naturally attract friends who appreciate you for who you are, your quirks, flaws, and everything else

What's To Come

In this chapter, I am going to show you how to attract true friendships just by being yourself. You don't have to change a thing. Sounds scary, but trust me, it works. The first step to becoming your authentic self is discovering who you are in the first place. That's where the concept of *self-awareness* comes in. It's about knowing who you are: your likes, dislikes, strengths, and the little things that make you tick. Once you know yourself, you can begin to embrace your authenticity. That's where true friendships begin.

Self-awareness isn't just about what you're good at or what you like. It's also knowing what throws you off, makes you uncomfortable, and what you need to feel good. Maybe you're an extrovert and get energy from being around people. Perhaps you're the opposite: an introvert, and you need some quiet time to recharge after hanging out with friends — both are totally okay. Understanding your nature will help you choose situations where you can shine, not just fit in.

I'll also provide you with some cool activities and quizzes to help you learn more about yourself. And hey, no need to stress; these aren't dull school tests. These tests are a fun way to dig deeper into who you really are. Plus, I'll give you tips on figuring out what your answers truly mean.

We'll also see how this self-understanding plays out in real life. For example, knowing your strengths can help you in conversations; understanding your boundaries can make your friendships stronger and more enjoyable — pretty cool, right?

And let's not overlook the online world. Your digital self is a big part of who you are. We'll explore how self-awareness can help you navigate social media and online interactions more confidently and authentically.

By the end of this chapter, you'll have a better grip on who you are. This knowledge is really important because the next step is learning how to face the things that scare you in social situations. But first, let's get to know you better.

GETTING TO KNOW YOURSELF

Think about the last time you felt comfortable in a group. Maybe you were chatting, laughing, or just hanging out, feeling like you belonged. You could be goofy and silly, put up your feet, and say whatever came to mind without worrying. You felt *at home*. It's fantastic, right?

Now, let's flip that feeling. Think of a time when you felt out of place or awkward in a group. Being uncomfortable in a group can make you feel like you're standing *in the spotlight*, but not in a good way. It's as though every eye is on you; every word you say and movement you make feels like it's under a magnifying glass. It seems as if you are holding your breath, and all you want more than anything is to exhale.

157

So, what made these experiences different? A big part of the answer lies in knowing yourself; that's what self-awareness is all about.

Self-awareness is like having a mental mirror. It's understanding your feelings, why you feel at home in some situations and why you want to crawl under a rock in others. Think of self-awareness as your personal user manual.

Why Self-Awareness Matters Before Mixing with Others

Why does self-awareness matter when you're around other people? Let's say you're at a party. If you know you get overwhelmed in big crowds, you can plan ahead. Maybe you can find a quiet space for a while or step outside to catch your breath. Knowing how to manage this challenge will help you handle the situation better.

This is exactly what happened to me. Everything changed when I began to understand my own tendencies through the process of self-awareness. At a friend's party where I was surrounded by music and animated conversations, I felt a mix of excitement and apprehension. Thanks to my growing self-awareness, I recognized my tendency to get overwhelmed in these situations.

Rather than diving into the thick of the party, I found a quiet corner to observe and take in the atmosphere at my own pace. This corner became my sanctuary, a place where I could breathe and recalibrate. As the evening progressed, I noticed the signs of rising anxiety and knew exactly when to step aside for a moment of solitude.

This approach wasn't just about managing my anxiety; it positively influenced the quality of my interactions. When I felt more centered and in control, my conversations were more authentic.

Taking these brief pauses to recharge didn't turn me into a snob; instead, they gave me the energy to re-engage with people meaningfully.

Do you see how the party turned into an opportunity for self-discovery? I learned to pay attention to how I felt and what I needed to feel better, making the party less intimidating and more enjoyable.

The Benefits of Self-Awareness

You Can Play to Your Strengths

Self-awareness is not just about managing the tough stuff like overwhelming crowds; it's also about learning how to play to your strengths. If you're good at listening, you might find that people love talking to you one-on-one. Recognizing this skill can make you more confident in social settings.

You Can Relate Better to Others

Self-awareness isn't just about you; it affects how you relate to others. Understanding your feelings makes you less likely to project them onto someone else. Say, for example, you're having a bad day. If you're self-aware, you know your mood might make you more sensitive. So, when a friend makes a joke, you're less likely to take it the wrong way.

You Can Empathize with Others

Self-awareness helps you to understand others better. When you know your emotions and reactions, you notice them in other people. This knowledge can make you a more empathetic friend who recognizes when a friend struggles, even if they don't verbalize the challenge.

There's an incredible ripple effect to self-awareness. The more you get it, the more you see it in the world around you. You'll start to understand why people do what they do. This doesn't mean you'll agree with everyone or like everything they do, but it will help you get where they're coming from.

Now, think about self-awareness as a skill. It's not something you're born with; it's something you can get better at. It's like learning to ride a bike. At first, you might wobble and fall. But the more you practice, the steadier you get. Like the bike, the more you work on self-awareness, the more natural it becomes.

Three Ways to Build Self-Awareness

How do you get better at self-awareness?

1. Check In with Your Mood: Start by paying attention to your feelings. When you're in a great mood, ask yourself what's making you feel that way. Do the same when you're having a bad day. It's like being a detective in your own life. The clues are already there; you just need to look for them.

2. Get Uncomfortable: Another way to build self-awareness is to experiment by stepping out of your comfort zone. Pay attention to how you react in these situations. You might discover you're braver than you thought or find joy in something you never knew you liked.

3. Listen Up: Make sure to listen to feedback. It's not always easy to hear what others have to say about us, but hearing their perspective can be incredibly valuable. Others may see something you are missing. Just remember to take feedback with a grain of salt. Not all feedback is accurate, but it can still contribute to the big picture of understanding yourself.

In the end, self-awareness is your secret weapon in our social world. It helps you understand yourself, which in turn helps you understand others. It's not about changing who you are to fit in. It's about knowing who you are so you can find where you fit. And that's a powerful thing.

SELF-DISCOVERY ACTIVITIES AND QUIZZES

Exploring your true self is a journey that's as enjoyable as diving into a new game or hobby. On the following pages, you'll find activities and quizzes that are crafted to guide you on this adventure of self-discovery.

Ten Activities for Self-Discovery

Feel free to spend as much time as you need on the activities below, whether it's just a day or an entire week. The key is to go at your own pace, savoring each experience. Begin with one activity, take your time, and work your way through the list whenever you're ready.

1. The Mood Tracker: For one week, jot down your mood at different times of the day. Are you happy, annoyed, excited, or nervous? Whatever the mood, write it down.

At the end of the week, look for patterns. Do certain things always make you feel overwhelmed or stressed? This activity helps you see what affects your mood.

Feelings Wheel

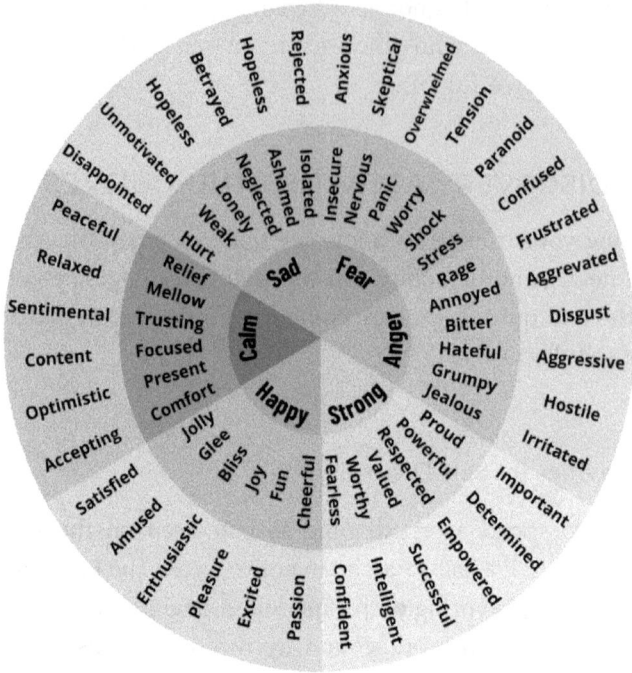

@ReallyGreatSite

2. The Compliment Reflection: Ask five people you trust to tell you what they think your strengths are and write them down. Do you see a common theme? This activity is excellent for understanding how others see your strengths.

3. The Dream Job Quiz: Create a list of jobs. Pick some you think are special and others at random. Then, choose your top three and explain why. This quiz can show you what you value in a career: creativity, helping others, or maybe problem-solving.

• • •

4. **The Friendship Map:** Draw a map of your friendships. Put yourself in the center and draw lines to your friends. The closer the friend, the closer they are to the center. This visual can help you understand your social circle and the kinds of friendships you have.

5. **The *What If* Game:** Write down ten what-if scenarios. What if you won a million dollars? What if you could travel anywhere? Your answers can reveal a lot about your hopes, fears, and dreams.

6. **The Alone Time Analysis:** Spend a day by yourself doing things you enjoy. At the end of the day, think about how you felt. Were you relaxed, bored, lonely, or something else? This analysis can tell you a lot about how much alone time you need and what activities you genuinely enjoy.

7. **The Change Challenge:** Think of one small thing you'd like to change about yourself and try it for a week. Maybe you can wake up earlier or drink more water. Notice how this change makes you feel and what it says about your ability to adapt and grow.

8. **The Passion Project:** Dedicate some time to engage in activities or hobbies that genuinely excite you. Whether it's painting, coding, or playing a musical instrument, immersing yourself in activities you're passionate about can reveal hidden aspects of yourself and what brings you joy.

9. **The Role Model Reflection:** List any three people you admire, whether famous or not. Write down why you admire them. This

activity can show you qualities you value and might want to develop yourself.

10. The Future Letter: Write a letter to your future self five years from now. What do you hope to tell them? This letter can be a powerful way to understand your dreams and goals.

As you do these activities, remember there's no right or wrong answer; they're about exploring and understanding yourself. Enjoy the process of self-discovery, and you might just find out some pretty cool things about who you are.

Self-Awareness Quiz

Another way you can get to know yourself is by examining how you handle challenging situations. Take a look at the questions below and answer them honestly. Choose the response that best reflects your feelings or preferences. At the end, I'll provide insights into what your answers might reveal about you. Let's begin.

1. How do you typically react in tough situations?

a. Keep calm and think it through

b. Hit up friends for advice

c. Feel overwhelmed and stressed

d. Dive right in and see what happens

2. What brings a big smile to your face?

a. Getting creative, like drawing or writing

b. Helping friends or volunteering

c. Competitive sports or games

d. Solving problems or cracking puzzles

3. How do you handle criticism or feedback?

a. Reflect on it and look for areas to improve

b. Appreciate different perspectives and consider making changes

c. Feel hurt or defensive

d. Disregard it and trust your instincts

4. What type of social situations do you find most enjoyable?

a. Intimate gatherings with close friends

b. Collaborative group activities

c. Energetic and bustling events

d. One-on-one conversations

5. What's your time management style?

a. Make lists and prioritize tasks

b. Rely on schedules and planners

c. Struggle to meet deadlines

d. Wing it and go with the flow

• • •

6. What is your approach to decision-making?

a. Think it through carefully

b. Gather opinions; the more, the merrier

c. Indecisiveness or avoidance

d. Trusting instincts and making quick decisions

7. What do you value most in your relationships with others?

a. Loyalty and trustworthiness

b. Open communication and understanding

c. Spontaneity and fun

d. Independence and personal space

Now, let's unpack what your answers might reveal about you. Each choice reflects aspects of your personality, preferences, and how you navigate challenges. These insights will give you a clearer picture of yourself and maybe uncover some interesting things you didn't know about yourself.

Mostly A's: Your thoughtful and organized approach suggests that you are likely to be self-aware. Keep rocking those analytical skills!

Mostly B's: You are a team player. You love bouncing ideas off others and value different perspectives. Teamwork makes the dream work, right?

Mostly C's: Stressful situations and criticism can be tricky, but don't worry, this is very common. Time to explore some stress-busting tricks and boost that confidence.

Mostly D's: Your quick decision-making and spontaneous nature suggest a strong sense of confidence and independence. While this can be an asset, it may also be helpful to reflect on situations more deeply at times to enhance self-awareness.

Feel free to return to this quiz every couple of months to see how much you've grown and changed.

THE RIPPLE EFFECT: HOW KNOWING YOURSELF AFFECTS YOUR CONNECTION TO OTHERS

Understanding yourself is like setting the stage before the main act in a play. It shapes how you interact with the world, especially with people around you. When you have a clear picture of who you are, you have a roadmap for navigating social situations. This clarity makes your life easier and improves the way you connect with others.

Setting Personal Boundaries

When I was a teenager, I had a best friend named Lauren. She always felt worn out after hanging out with friends. At first, Lauren couldn't figure out why. She liked her friends and enjoyed their company, but she felt drained whenever she left a big get-together. It was like running a marathon without any training. After some self-observation, Lauren realized she was an introvert. Big groups and long social gatherings were exhausting for her, and she needed time alone to recharge her batteries.

With this new understanding, Lauren changed how she approached social events by setting personal boundaries. She didn't stop hanging out with me or her other friends; instead, she found ways to balance her social life with her need for alone time. Just like how I found a quiet corner to regroup at parties, Lauren also made a plan for herself. She would join her friends and hang out for a bit, but then she would leave a bit earlier than everyone else when things felt overwhelming.

These small changes added up to a big impact. Lauren's friends and I began to understand her better. We didn't see her early exits as rude; instead, we understood it was how Lauren took care of herself. By being open about her needs, Lauren helped us better understand her. Her personal development made her friendships stronger and more respectful of her limits.

Lauren's story is a perfect example of the ripple effect of self-awareness. By understanding her own needs, she was able to communicate them to others, leading to more enjoyable and meaningful social interactions. Self-discovery is about finding a balance that works for you and those around you.

The key takeaway is simple yet powerful: When you know yourself, you can set boundaries to bring peace to your life and enrich your interactions with others. You stay true to yourself and build stronger, more genuine connections — a win-win situation.

Understanding Emotional Triggers

Another part of self-awareness that greatly affects our interactions with others is *recognizing emotional triggers*. These triggers are specific actions that set off strong emotions in us, often unexpectedly. Understanding these triggers can dramatically improve our social interactions and relationships.

My brother Tom always got defensive and upset whenever someone offered him criticism. This reaction was as automatic as a switch being flipped. It didn't matter if the criticism was gentle or harsh. Tom's immediate response was to push back, sometimes leading to arguments with friends or tense moments at school.

After some self-reflection, Tom began to understand that his reactions were tied to feelings from his past. Growing up, he often faced harsh criticism that made him feel inadequate. As a result, any criticism in the present, even well-intended, triggered old feelings of not being good enough.

This realization was a turning point for Tom. He started to work on responding differently to criticism. Instead of immediately getting defensive, he learned to take a moment, breathe, and remind himself that not all criticism is an attack on his character. This realization didn't happen overnight; it took practice and patience. Gradually, Tom could listen to constructive feedback without feeling personally attacked.

This shift in Tom's behavior significantly impacted his social life. His friends noticed he was more open and took time before any necessary argument. This shift made their interactions more pleasant and constructive. Tom's new approach helped him learn and grow from feedback at home and school instead of shutting it down.

Tom's transformation shows the power of understanding emotional triggers. By recognizing and working on these triggers, we can improve our reactions in social situations. This recognition leads to healthier and more fulfilling relationships. It also helps us to communicate more effectively, as we're no longer battling unseen emotional responses from our past.

STRENGTHS AND WEAKNESSES

One of the most empowering parts of self-awareness is identifying your strengths and weaknesses. It's about taking a look at what you're naturally good at and what areas could use improvement. This understanding shapes how you interact with others, turning everyday social experiences into opportunities for growth and connection.

As a teen, I felt extremely uneasy making small talk. The idea of chatting about the weather or what someone did over the weekend always felt awkward and forced to me. However, I came to understand that I had a unique gift: I was an excellent listener. When someone talked to me, I always paid full attention, showing genuine interest in their words. This ability made people feel heard and valued when they spoke with me.

After acknowledging this new information, I decided to lean into my strength. Instead of forcing myself to make small talk, I would ask open-ended questions that let others do more of the talking — this approach worked wonders. People enjoyed conversations with me because they felt I truly listened and engaged with what they said. My friends and peers began to see me as a go-to person for advice and meaningful conversations. The pressure of making conversations was lifted right off of my shoulders.

By focusing on my strength as a listener, I turned what I saw as a social weakness – my struggle with small talk – into a unique power. This shift didn't just change how I interacted with others; it also changed how I saw myself. I became more confident in social settings, knowing I had a valuable skill to offer in my interactions.

Identifying Strengths and Weaknesses

Identifying your strengths and weaknesses is not about labeling yourself as good or bad at certain things; it's about knowing your personal toolkit. Your strengths are your tools, something you can use to build positive experiences and relationships. Your weaknesses, on the other hand, are areas where you might need to pick up some new tools or skills.

So, how do you go about identifying your positive attributes and areas for improvement? Begin by reflecting on your recent interactions. Think about times when you felt comfortable (a.k .a. feeling *at home*) and times when you felt out of your element (a.k .a. feeling *under the spotlight*). What were you doing in each situation? This information can give you clues about your natural strengths and areas for growth.

How This Knowledge Can Boost Your Social Life

Once you understand your strengths and weaknesses, you can use them to your advantage in social situations. Like me, you can play to your strengths and find ways to work around your weaknesses. Maybe you're great at making people laugh but struggle to open up about your feelings. You could use your humor to ease into more personal conversations gradually.

Identifying your strengths and weaknesses can also help you choose activities where you can thrive. If you know you're great at organizing and leading, you might enjoy being part of a club or a team. If you're more of a creative thinker who likes to work independently, you might shine in activities like writing or art. Conversely, when you lean into areas that are challenging, you can make your social experiences more fulfilling and well-rounded.

THE JOY IN SELF-AWARENESS

Knowing what makes you happy is a crucial part of self-awareness, especially in shaping your social life. When you know what brings you joy, you can seek out experiences and relationships that resonate with your true self. This alignment enhances your happiness and enriches your interactions with others.

Finding What Brought Me Joy

When I was a teenager, I was someone who always went along with my friends to loud, crowded hangouts. Despite the fun atmosphere, I found very little enjoyment in these events. Even with stepping out for breaks, I still felt overwhelmed by the noise and the crowd. It wasn't that I didn't like my friends or being social; it was the setting that didn't suit me.

When I started reflecting on my feelings, I realized I preferred quieter, more intimate gatherings. I enjoyed deep conversations and shared experiences in a more relaxed environment. With this recognition, I started to change the way I socialized. Instead of trying to fit into the party scene, I began organizing movie nights and dinner gatherings at my place. These events were more in line with what I enjoyed: a comfortable setting where I could connect with friends on a deeper level.

This change made a significant difference in my social life. My friends got to see a different side of me. They enjoyed the calm, cozy atmosphere of my movie nights and the personal touch of my dinner parties. These gatherings allowed for conversations and bonding that the noisy hangouts didn't provide. My friends appreciated this new way of hanging out (complete with sweat-pants and Netflix), and I looked forward to these get-togethers. By the way, even years later, I continue to host monthly movie nights with my friends.

Find What Brings You Joy

Understanding what makes you happy in social settings is not about avoiding socializing or being different from others; it's about finding settings where you can be your best self. You're more relaxed, open, and genuine in a setting that aligns with your happiness. This authenticity draws people to you and helps build stronger, more meaningful connections.

Start noticing the environments where you feel most at ease or *at home* and those where you feel out of place or *under the spotlight*. Reflect on the activities that bring you joy and those that don't. It's also helpful to try new things. Sometimes, you might discover a new source of happiness in an unexpected place.

Remember, what makes you happy might differ from what makes others happy — that's perfectly okay. Embracing these differences can transform your social experiences. Your identity allows you to engage in activities that bring out the best in you and form connections with others who appreciate your authentic self.

SELF-AWARENESS LEADS TO AUTHENTICITY

Authenticity, the art of being your true self, could be the most valuable gift of self-awareness. Authenticity sheds the layers of expectations and norms to reveal who you truly are. When you're authentic, you connect with others on a deeper, more meaningful level — just like Emily did.

Emily's Story

Like so many teens her age, Emily spent years molding herself to fit in. She liked what her friends liked, dressed how they dressed, and even adjusted her opinions to match theirs. On the surface, these efforts seemed to work. She became a part of the group, always involved in their activities. But deep down, Emily felt a void. She was like an actor playing a role; the stage was her life, and the performance never ended.

The turning point for Emily came when she began exploring her interests. She started small by reading books that intrigued her, not just the ones her friends discussed. She explored music beyond the top charts, finding bands and genres that resonated with her. Emily also explored different looks, opting for outfits that brought her comfort and joy rather than following current trends.

Figuring out who she was not always smooth sailing for Emily. At first, she worried about what her friends would think. Would they judge her? Would she still fit in? But as Emily embraced her true self, she started seeing big changes in her life. Emily started attracting people who liked her for who she was, not who she was trying to be. Her conversations became more engaging and fulfilling because they were genuine. Emily found friends with whom she shared real interests, leading to deeper connections and more enjoyable social experiences.

174

Emily's story is a testament to the power of authenticity. Being true to yourself isn't just about personal happiness; it's about the quality of your relationships. Authentic people attract others who are genuine, which in turn creates a circle of trust and openness.

How to Become More Authentic

How can you start being more authentic? First, spend time with yourself. Work on the *Ten Activities for Self-Discovery* listed at the beginning of this chapter. Get to know your likes, dislikes, and values. What excites you? What do you believe in? Once you start figuring out who you are, you can begin expressing these aspects of yourself in your daily life. Speak your mind respectfully, choose activities that align with your interests, and don't be afraid to show your unique style.

Remember, authenticity isn't about being different for the sake of it; It's being true to yourself. You don't have to reject everything popular or mainstream. Instead, choose what resonates with you, regardless of whether it's trendy or unconventional.

Being authentic means being open to growth and change. As you go through life, your interests and values might evolve, and that's okay. Accept these changes as part of the process. Authenticity is not static; it's about embracing your identity at every stage of your life.

THE DIGITAL YOU – SELF-AWARENESS IN THE ONLINE WORLD

In today's digital age, our online presence is as much a part of our identity as our physical presence. Self-awareness extends beyond the physical world into the realm of social media, online gaming, and virtual classrooms. Understanding how you present yourself online and how that image aligns with your real-world persona is vital for authentic interactions — on and off the screen.

Digital Self-Awareness: Social Media

The digital world offers a unique platform where you can express yourself, share your thoughts, and connect with others. Unfortunately, it's also a place where it's easy to lose sight of who you are. In the world of likes, shares, and follows, it's tempting to create an online persona that's more about getting approval from others than expressing your true self. This is where self-awareness comes in. You need to be mindful of the image you're projecting online and ensure it reflects your genuine self.

It's important to distinguish between genuine interactions and merely chasing after likes. Finding that balance and keeping it real online helps you make meaningful connections and preserves your sense of self in the digital landscape. Embracing self-awareness in the social media world gives you the power to navigate it with purpose and honesty.

Digital Self-Awareness: Online Gaming

Online gaming is another digital space where self-awareness plays a key role. It's a space where you can cultivate any character and interact with others in a virtual environment. While online gaming is a great way to escape reality and have fun, staying mindful of how much of your real self you bring into these games is essential.

Remember that it's essential to check in and make sure you're not using gaming to avoid things in your real life. Are you using gaming to express parts of your personality you might be holding back in the real world? Or is it a way to disconnect entirely from who you are? Balancing the fun of gaming with a clear understanding of why you're doing it helps you enjoy the virtual world without losing touch with the real one.

Digital Self-Awareness: Virtual Classes

Virtual classes and learning environments also require self-awareness. Focus on being conscious of how you engage with others in these settings. Are you participating and contributing in a way that reflects your true interest and investment in the subject? Are you respectful and considerate in your interactions, just as in a physical classroom? Being self-aware in these environments ensures that you will get the most out of your online learning experience while being a positive presence for others.

Knowing when to take breaks, handle distractions, and communicate effectively adds to a smoother and more enjoyable online learning experience. This awareness of your own needs and habits is just part of being *in the know* about yourself. It helps you adapt your approach to online learning, stay focused, and create an environment that suits your learning style.

Creating an Authentic Digital Identity

Self-awareness in the digital realm is about aligning your online presence with your true self. It's about being mindful of how you interact in these spaces and ensuring that your digital footprint genuinely reflects you. By being self-aware online, you create a digital identity that is authentic, respectful, and true to who you are, enhancing both your virtual and real-world relationships.

Here are four ways to align your online persona with your real-life personality.

1. Be Mindful of What you Post: Before sharing something, ask yourself if the content genuinely reflects your thoughts, feelings, or experiences. Consider the motivations behind your posts. Are you sharing something because it's important to you, or are you seeking validation and approval from others?

2. Let it Evolve: It's okay for your online persona to evolve as you grow and change in real life. Your online presence can reflect these changes as you learn more about yourself, your interests, and your values.

3. Match Up Your Worlds: Consider how your online interactions affect your real-world relationships. If you're kind and supportive online, carry those traits into your real-life interactions. Similarly, if you find yourself being more negative or critical online, reflect on those actions and how they could impact your relationships and mental well-being.

4. Take a Breather: Take breaks from the online world to connect with yourself and others in real life. These breaks will help maintain a balanced perspective and ensure your online persona doesn't overshadow your real-life experiences and relationships.

———

Now that we've explored self-awareness, from understanding your strengths and weaknesses to aligning your real-life personality with your digital persona, we stand at a significant crossroads. The path ahead is about moving beyond mere awareness to actively overcoming the barriers that hold you back in social settings — obstacles like fear and shyness.

Let's embark on this next exciting phase, where self-awareness becomes the springboard for conquering personal obstacles and thriving in your social world.

CHAPTER 2

OVERCOMING OBSTACLES (O)

> "Courage is not the absence of fear, but the triumph over it." – Nelson Mandela

Let's face it: even the bravest among us face fears. In this chapter, you'll embark on a journey to identify and understand these fears. Is it shyness that makes you blend into the background? Anxiety that makes your heart race in social settings? Or is it a fear of saying the wrong thing that keeps your thoughts locked inside? Recognizing these fears is the first step towards overcoming them.

Identification alone isn't enough. I will also show you effective techniques to conquer these obstacles. From cognitive behavioral therapy (CBT) methods that challenge and change your thought patterns to mindfulness techniques that help you stay grounded and calm in the moment, you'll discover tools that can transform your approach to social situations.

Building confidence is the final step to crushing those social hurdles. Confidence is like a muscle; the more you use it, the stronger it becomes. You'll explore ways to develop confidence, understanding how it can change how you view yourself and how others perceive you. Confidence doesn't mean you won't ever feel afraid; it means you'll have the strength to face your fears and thrive despite them.

This chapter also includes real-life examples and case studies. These stories of triumph over social anxieties will inspire you and show that change is possible and within reach.

Overcoming social obstacles is a process, a journey towards a more confident and fulfilling social life. As you turn these pages, you're taking steps towards breaking down the barriers of fear and shyness, paving the way for richer, more enjoyable social experiences.

IDENTIFYING FEARS, SHYNESS, AND SOCIAL ANXIETY

The journey to overcoming social fears begins with a crucial first step: identifying and acknowledging these fears. Social fears come in various forms, including a general sense of shyness and specific social anxieties. Let's explore these specific areas and uncover how they might manifest in your life.

Shyness

For many, *shyness* is like a quiet shadow lurking behind in social situations. Shyness is not always about fear but more about feeling uncomfortable or unsure when the spotlight turns your way. This shyness can manifest in avoiding eye contact, staying quiet in groups, or feeling uneasy in new social settings. Shy people might have nervous habits like touching their faces or twirling their hair. Shyness is a form of self-consciousness, a worry about how others perceive you.

. . .

Social Anxiety

Social anxiety is an intense fear of being judged or embarrassed in social situations. This feeling can be so overpowering that it disrupts daily life. People with social anxiety might avoid social events altogether, experience significant anxiety at the thought of being in social situations, or exert a lot of effort to get through them. A person with social anxiety struggles in situations where they may be judged, such as meeting new people, answering a question in class, or having to talk to a cashier in a store.

Measuring Your Social Temperature

To help you identify your social comfort level, consider these questions inspired by the party concept:

1. When you think about attending a party, what feeling comes first?

- Excitement to meet new people.
- Nervousness about who you'll talk to.
- Dread at the thought of being in a crowd.
- Worry about being noticed or judged.

2. At a social gathering, where do you usually find yourself?

- Mingling and chatting with various people.
- Sticking close to one or two friends.
- Finding a quiet corner to observe from a distance.
- Looking for an excuse to leave early.

3. How do you feel about speaking in front of a group?

- It's a fun challenge.
- It's a bit nerve-wracking but manageable.
- It's incredibly uncomfortable, but you can push through it.
- It's your worst nightmare and to be avoided at all costs.

4. How do you feel about making small talk?

- Enjoy it and find it effortless.
- Do it when necessary but prefer deeper conversations.
- Feel awkward and struggle to keep the conversation going.
- Dread it and often find ways to avoid it.

5. How do you react to being the center of the group's focus?

- Embrace it and enjoy being in the spotlight.
- Feel a bit uncomfortable but manage to navigate it.
- Experience heightened anxiety and seek ways to redirect attention.
- Find it distressing and immediately try to retreat from the spotlight.

Your responses can help pinpoint the degree of social discomfort you experience. For example, did you choose answers that show slight discomfort in group settings, or did they reveal a more intense fear around social situations? There are no right or wrong answers. In the following sections, we'll explore strategies to help you overcome social challenges, big and small.

TECHNIQUES FOR OVERCOMING SOCIAL OBSTACLES

Overcoming social fears and anxieties is a journey that requires both understanding and action. Two effective methods to manage and conquer these fears are *cognitive behavioral therapy* (CBT) and *mindfulness*. Both offer practical strategies that can be applied in daily life to gradually reduce the impact of social fears.

Cognitive Behavioral Therapy (CBT) for Social Fears

Cognitive behavioral therapy is a type of therapy that shows how our thoughts, feelings, and actions are all connected. Here's an interesting fact: Did you know that thousands of negative thoughts run through our minds on a daily basis? Yes, thousands! These negative thoughts can lead to negative emotions, affecting our behavior in social situations. But here's the cool part—if you flip those thoughts, you can change how you feel and act in social situations. It's like giving your mind a makeover.

For example, if you think, *"I'm going to say something stupid,"* this thought might make you feel anxious, leading you to avoid social interactions altogether. CBT works by challenging and replacing this thought with a more balanced one, such as, *"Everyone makes mistakes in conversation sometimes — it's normal."*

Thought Records

One very simple and effective CBT exercise is called *thought records*. Thought records help you figure out and change those pesky negative thoughts that can bring you down. Imagine it as a way to understand what's going on in your mind when you're feeling upset. Keeping track of your thoughts helps with self-awareness and stops negative thoughts in their tracks.

Here's how it works. Keep a journal of negative thoughts you have about social situations. Write down the *situation*, the *thought*, the *emotion* it triggered, and how you *reacted*. In the end, try to come up with a more balanced thought for the same situation.

Step-by-Step Guide for Thought Records:

1. **Date and Time:** Jot down exactly when this event happened.

· · ·

2. **Situation/Trigger:** Describe the specific situation that led to your negative thoughts and emotions. Be detailed and specific.

3. **Mood/Emotion:** Use the feelings wheel from Chapter 1 to track your mood. Rate your feelings on a scale from 1-10, with 1 having little intensity and 10 being extremely intense.

4. **Automatic Negative Thoughts (ANTs):** Write down the thoughts that instantly popped up when things got tough.

5. **Evidence Supporting ANTs:** Look at the facts that support those automatic thoughts. Are they based on anything true?

6. **Evidence Against ANTs:** Find any proof that doesn't agree with those automatic thoughts. See if there's another side to the story.

7. **Alternative, Balanced Thoughts:** Come up with more helpful thoughts that are less negative and more realistic.

8. **Re-Rate Your Mood/Emotion:** Check back on your feelings after thinking about things in a new way. Re-rate the intensity of your feelings on a scale from 1-10. Did anything change?

By going through this process, you can learn a lot about your thought patterns, challenge irrational beliefs, and develop healthier, more balanced thinking. The goal is to understand your thoughts better and find ways to make them more positive and balanced. You can use this tool with a therapist, or even on your own to help deal with tough emotions.

. . .

Thought Record in Real-Time

Date and Time: *December 15, 2023, 3:30 PM*

Situation/Trigger: *During the group project meeting in the library, I had to share my ideas for the presentation. Everyone was looking at me, and I felt extremely nervous about being judged.*

Mood/Emotion: *Using the feelings wheel, I'd say my mood was mostly anxious and a bit embarrassed. I'd rate it around a 7, feeling pretty intense.*

Automatic Negative Thoughts (ANTS): *They all think my ideas are dumb. I'm going to mess up the presentation, and everyone will remember it.*

Evidence Supporting ANTS: *Well, some people seemed unimpressed when I was talking. Plus, I stumbled on my words, which made me feel like they were judging me.*

Evidence Against ANTS: *But, not everyone looked uninterested, and some were nodding as if they understood. Plus, I know I've got good ideas; it's just the nerves talking.*

Alternative, Balanced Thoughts: *I might not have aced the presentation today, but it doesn't mean all my ideas are bad. I can improve, and everyone has off days.*

Re-Rate Your Mood/Emotion: *After thinking about it differently, my anxiety dropped a bit. I'd say it's more like a 5 now. I still feel a bit embarrassed, but it's not as overwhelming as before.*

Do you see how using a thought record in real-life situations can be incredibly helpful, shifting negative thoughts, managing emotions, and promoting a more balanced perspective in overcoming social anxiety? Now, let's look at how *mindfulness* can also help overcome social obstacles.

. . .

Mindfulness for Social Anxiety

Another technique for overcoming social obstacles is *mindfulness*. Mindfulness involves staying present and fully engaged in the current moment without judgment. It's about noticing your thoughts and feelings without getting caught up in them. Mindfulness can be particularly helpful in managing the physical symptoms of social anxiety like increased heart rate or sweating.

Here are some daily mindfulness tips:

- **Mindful Breathing**: Whenever you feel anxious, focus on your breath. Take slow, deep breaths, and pay attention to the sensation of air moving in and out of your body.

- **Progressive Muscle Relaxation**: Systematically tense and then release each muscle group in your body. First, tighten up your fists, then let them go and relax. Next, move to your shoulders and then travel through each muscle group from your toes to your head. This activity is like a reset button for your body, helping you feel more relaxed and calm in social situations.

- **Grounding Techniques:** When in a social setting, ground yourself by feeling the sensation of your feet on the floor. This helps you stay present and connected to the environment.

- **Five Senses Check-In:** Take a moment to engage each of your five senses. Identify five things you can see, four things you can touch, three things you can hear, two things you can smell, and one thing you can taste. This activity will bring your attention to the present moment.

- **Visual Anchoring:** Carry a small object with you, like a stone or a keychain, and use it as a visual anchor. When you feel anxious, hold the object and concentrate on its details to ground yourself in the present.

- **Finding Beauty in the Room:** Take a moment to find something beautiful in the room you're in. It could be a piece of artwork, a plant, or even the play of light. Pay close attention to the details, colors, and textures. Allow yourself to become absorbed in the beauty of this element, using it as a calming focal point in the midst of social situations.

- **Mindful Socializing**: Approach social interactions with a mindful mindset. Instead of worrying about how you are perceived, focus on the experience itself. Engage in the conversation without judgment, allowing it to unfold naturally.

Look through this list and circle three that you'd like to start right away. As you practice, check them off. Try using your thought record journal to keep track of what mindfulness activities you've tried and how it went.

Keep in mind that mindfulness is a skill that grows with regular practice over time. Incorporating these activities into your daily routine can help manage social anxiety and promote a sense of calmness in all social settings.

As you keep up with CBT and mindfulness techniques, you'll start to get the hang of calming yourself down and tweaking the thoughts and actions that feed into your worries. Your confidence in social situations will grow as you use these methods consistently. And the great news? This increased sense of ease can open up many social opportunities that used to be overshadowed by fear and anxiety. You're on your way to mastering this!

CULTIVATING CONFIDENCE FOR SOCIAL SUCCESS

Confidence is a cornerstone in overcoming social fears and making interactions with people easier. It's so much more than just feeling good about yourself; it's a key part of navigating social situations. Confidence can transform how we approach social situations, how we communicate, and even how we perceive and are perceived by others.

As highlighted in my first book, *The Confident Teen*, when you're confident, you feel sure of yourself and believe in your abilities, even in the face of tough challenges. You also take pride in your individuality and your actions show that you embrace your quirks. But it's not about acting superior. It's about saying, "I *can do this*," and genuinely believing it in your heart. It doesn't stop there, though. Confidence also involves acting on that belief in yourself.

The most important thing to remember about confidence is that it's a skill you can improve with practice by building a confident mindset, comparing yourself kindly (because we all have our unique talents), and overcoming self-doubt.

Does being confident mean you'll never doubt yourself again?

Nope. Self-doubt will always find a way to creep in. Even the most confident people experience fear and uncertainty. Confidence just means pushing through and not allowing self-doubt to stop you from living life and being the best version of yourself.

Alex's Story

You have a friend, Alex, who struggles with social anxiety. Speaking in class or joining group discussions is a nightmare for him. Alex's fear of saying something wrong or being laughed at is so intense that he often remains silent, even when he has valuable contributions to make.

However, when Alex starts to focus on building his confidence, things begin to change. He starts with small steps, like participating in smaller group discussions, and gradually works his way up to speaking in front of the class. With each successful interaction, his confidence grows, and his social anxiety diminishes.

Alex's experience illustrates that you can build confidence by doing the very thing that scares you, little by little. Even if you're not feeling totally sure of yourself, you can still project a confident vibe, showing that you've got what it takes to navigate social situations with ease. In other words, *fake it until you make it.*

Rest assured, no one is born confident. It's a skill you can develop over time. By recognizing your strengths, setting boundaries, and believing in yourself, you can build the confidence to face social fears and flourish in social environments just like Alex. As we continue, we'll explore more specific strategies and exercises to help develop confidence, transforming how you interact with others and view yourself.

Building Confidence: Practical Tips and Strategies

Confidence is the key you need to navigate the complex world of social interactions. It opens doors, propels you forward, and empowers you to live without limits.

Here are some daily routines to help cultivate confidence. Just like with the self-discovery activities in Chapter 1, circle your favorite activity to start with, take your time, and work your way through the list at your own pace.

Daily Routines to Enhance Confidence

- **Morning Affirmations**: Start your day by looking in the mirror and saying positive statements about yourself. Stick some colorful post-it notes with empowering phrases on your mirror and say them out loud to set a positive tone.

Everything is going to be okay.

@ReallyGreatSite

- **Look Good, Feel Good**: Wear clothes that make you feel good about yourself. It's not about wearing expensive things. Spend a few extra minutes getting yourself ready in the morning. How you look can influence your mood and how you carry yourself.

- **Social Skills Practice**: Each day, challenge yourself to step out of your comfort zone in small ways. These steps could be speaking up in class, offering someone help, or asserting yourself with your latte order at Starbucks.

- **Practice Gratitude**: Every day, write down three things you're grateful for about yourself. These could include a skill, a quality, or an achievement. When I was a teen, I hated my acne, but I began appreciating my beautiful green eyes. My gratitude list was a reminder to pay attention to my awesome features.

- **Stay Active:** Get moving with physical activities you actually like. Exercise isn't just about staying fit; it's also a great mood booster. When exercising, happy hormones called endorphins are released, making you feel fantastic.

- **Confident Body Language:** Pay attention to your body language. Even if you feel insecure, no one needs to know it. Maintain good posture, make eye contact, and use open gestures. Confident body language sends positive signals to your brain, boosting a confident self-image.

How Confidence Affects How Others See You

Did you know that the way you present yourself speaks volumes? The way you conduct yourself and how you act is a direct reflection of how people see you. How you stand, make eye contact, and even talk can show off your confidence. And guess what? When you're rocking that confidence, people think you're capable, trustworthy, and easy to approach. Who wouldn't want that kind of magic?

Those who express their ideas confidently tend to be more influential in group settings. Their confidence can make their ideas more persuasive and can even elevate their social standing within the group.

Confidence isn't about being the loudest voice in the room; it's the quiet assurance that you are capable and worthy of respect. This self-assurance is often more compelling than mere words; it's a language that speaks through actions and demeanor.

Building confidence is a journey that involves changing how you think, act, and perceive yourself. By making those confidence routines a daily habit and remembering the impact of confidence on how others see you, you're slowly building a rock-solid foundation of self-assurance. This confidence will help you navigate social challenges and empower you to present your true self to the world.

THE ROLE OF EXTERNAL FACTORS IN SOCIAL ANXIETY

Having social anxiety isn't just about what's going on inside your head; a lot of it comes from what's happening around you. External factors like *social media* and *peer pressure* play a big role in making teens feel anxious in social situations. Recognizing how these outside influences impact you is the first step in breaking free from their hold.

Social Media's Impact

The rise of social media has brought about new challenges, especially for teens. Platforms such as *Instagram, Snapchat,* and *TikTok* are more than just spaces for sharing photos and videos; they have become arenas for social comparison. Seeing posts where peers are living seemingly perfect lives can amplify feelings of exclusion and loneliness. Looking at these kinds of posts non-stop can skew your idea of what's normal in social situations, making you feel even worse.

For example, have you ever scrolled through social media and found a friend's breathtaking hike through a lush forest, their radiant joy leaving you questioning why your life doesn't seem as adventurous? It hurts, doesn't it? Social media has a way of sparking this kind of self-doubt. In this era of presenting picture-perfect snapshots, it's only natural to compare yourself with others. But remember, those posts are carefully crafted, and they only capture a slice of the complete story.

. . .

Peer Pressure

Peer pressure is an extremely powerful force during adolescence. That desire to fit in and be accepted by your peers could push you to do things you're not okay with. It might even cause you to avoid situations entirely because you're worried about what your friends will think. This pressure can make you feel even more isolated and crank up your anxiety when you're in social settings.

It's like there's this unspoken rulebook, and everyone's trying to keep up. The fear of standing out or being judged can be intense, pushing you to follow the crowd even if it feels wrong. And when you don't go along with the group, that worry about being the odd one out can be overwhelming. It's important to remember that it's okay to listen to your gut and do what's best for you. Don't worry; genuine friends will respect your choices, while others can naturally fade away. In the following pages, I will show you exactly how to lighten the load of peer pressure.

MINIMIZING THE IMPACT OF EXTERNAL FACTORS

While we cannot always control the external factors contributing to social anxiety, we can take steps to minimize their impact on our lives. Here are some practical tips to manage these external influences:

Loosen the Grip of Social Media

Social media can be a double-edged sword. It offers opportunities for connection and expression but can also be a source of anxiety. Setting boundaries is imperative; here are some tips:

- Limit your time on social platforms and designate specific times of the day for social media.

- Avoid scrolling through social media just before bed or first thing in the morning. These times are when your mind is most impressionable.

- Be selective about who you follow. Choose to follow accounts that inspire and uplift you rather than those that fuel comparison and inadequacy.

Keep in mind that social media only gives us a polished snapshot of life; it's far from the real picture. Scrolling through those perfectly filtered photos and glamorous posts will almost always lead to self-doubt. Don't get tricked by the flawless images on social media. Behind those posts are real people with their own challenges and doubts. Comparing your life to those idealized images is unfair to you. Remember, those posts are only a small piece of their actual story.

Instead of getting caught in the comparison trap, shift your mindset. Celebrate what makes you unique: your talents, passions, and experiences. Life isn't about who's better than who; it's about embracing your own growth, progress, and individuality.

Loosen the Grip of Peer Pressure

A solid support network of friends and family who will have your back no matter what can help with the stress caused by peer pressure. Having people who care about you and support you unconditionally will give you a safe space to express your feelings and fears. Open communication within this circle can help address issues before they escalate. Here's how to build and maintain a strong support network:

- **Identify Your Support Circle**: Think about the people in your life who make you feel heard and understood. They can include family members, friends, teachers, or mentors.

- **Cultivate Open Communication**: Encourage honest and open conversations within this group. Share your thoughts and feelings and make yourself available to listen in return.

- **Seek Diverse Perspectives**: Having a variety of viewpoints in your support network can help you see different aspects of a situation, making it easier to find balanced solutions to problems.

- **Regular Check-Ins**: Stay in touch with your support network regularly. Whether it's a text or a call, keeping up with these interactions can strengthen your bonds and ensure ongoing support.

––––––

Having worked on overcoming fears and anxieties, you are now better equipped for the next part of our journey: engaging in conversations.

Conversations are the bridges that connect us as humans. They are the tools through which we share ideas, express feelings, and build relationships. But how do you make these interactions not just possible but also enjoyable and fulfilling?

The next chapter will explore the nuances of conversation skills. You'll learn about starting and maintaining conversations, the art of listening, and how to express yourself clearly and confidently. These skills are vital for creating meaningful bonds with others.

Like overcoming social fears, mastering conversation skills requires patience and practice. You will build on your established foundation and expand your social toolkit. With each step, you'll find that conversations become less daunting and more enjoyable.

Let's get ready to fine-tune your conversation skills and turn those social interactions from nerve-wracking experiences to enjoyable realities.

CHAPTER 3
CRAFT CONFIDENT CONVERSATIONS (C)

> "The art of conversation is the art of hearing as well as of being heard." – William Hazlitt

Conversations can be tricky, can't they? Sometimes, you want to talk but don't know what to say. You feel lost for words or overwhelmed by what to say next. Other times, you might be talking but feel like no one's listening. Or maybe you're listening but can't find the right moment to chime in — sound familiar? Well, you're not alone. At some point, everyone faces these hurdles.

In this chapter, you'll discover how to start a chat, keep it interesting, and leave a positive impression, all while being true to yourself. You'll also learn how to be a good listener, a skill as important as speaking. After all, conversations are a two-way street.

You're about to unlock the secrets of turning awkward silences into opportunities, transforming nervousness into confidence, and making every chat enjoyable. Conversation is not just talking; it's about connecting, understanding, and being understood. Let's turn those awkward moments into stories of triumph, one conversation at a time.

LAYING THE GROUNDWORK FOR GREAT CONVERSATION

Chatting with someone feels great when the conversation flows naturally and we feel heard and understood. Unfortunately, there are times when conversations can feel like a bumpy road, leaving us unsure or even a bit frustrated. So, what sets apart a good discussion from a not-so-great one? Let's take a closer look.

Good Conversations

Think about a time when you had a great chat with someone. Maybe you both lost track of time because you were so engaged; that's the magic of a good conversation. In these interactions, both people listen attentively by showing genuine interest in the other person's words. It's like a rhythmic dance of dialogue, where thoughts and ideas flow seamlessly between both people, creating an enriching exchange.

In these conversations, it's not just about talking — it's connecting. You feel comfortable and excited to share your thoughts because you know the other person is truly listening. They might ask questions to show they care or share something about themselves, which creates a bond. It's a give-and-take where both people contribute and respect each other's views, even if they differ.

Bad Conversations

Now, let's switch gears to those conversations that aren't as productive. Imagine talking to someone who seems more interested in their phone than in what you're saying. Or maybe you can't get a word in because they keep talking over you. These are signs of an unproductive conversation.

In bad conversations, one person might dominate the talk, leaving the other feeling like a spectator rather than a participant. Sometimes, it feels like you're not even having the same conversation. You might be discussing your weekend plans; suddenly, the other person shifts to something completely different. This shift is frustrating, making you feel undervalued.

TURNING BAD INTO GOOD: AVOIDING COMMON PITFALLS

How do we turn a potentially awful conversation into a good one? The key is to identify conversation pitfalls and learn how to avoid them.

Recognizing Common Conversation Mistakes

- **Interrupting**: Cutting someone off mid-sentence is a frequent misstep. Interrupting can make the other person feel undervalued and frustrated. It disrupts the flow of conversation and can even ruin the opportunity to make new friends.

- **Oversharing**: Sharing too much information, especially personal details, can make others uncomfortable. It's important to gauge the situation and your intimacy level with the other person.

- **Not Listening:** Failing to listen attentively is a common mistake. Sometimes, we're so focused on what we want to say next that we don't fully engage with what the other person is saying.

- **Dominating the Conversation:** Hogging the spotlight and not allowing others to get a word in can make the conversation one-sided. A good conversation is a balanced exchange of ideas.

Remedies for Conversation Pitfalls

For Interrupting:

- **Pause Before Responding:** Train yourself to wait a few seconds after the other person finishes speaking before you begin.

- **Acknowledge if You Interrupt:** If you catch yourself interrupting, apologize and encourage the other person to continue.

For Oversharing:

- **Read the Room**: Gauge the comfort level of the other person. Share personal details only when appropriate.

- **Balance Sharing:** Make sure that the sharing is mutual. If you're dominating the conversation, step back and encourage the other person to share.

For Not Listening:

- **Pay Full Attention:** Fully focus on the speaker, nodding and giving verbal affirmations.

- **Reflect:** Paraphrase or summarize what the other person has said to show that you've been listening.

For Dominating the Conversation:

- **Ask Open-Ended Questions:** Encourage the other person to talk more by asking questions that require more than a *yes* or *no* answer.

- **Be Conscious of Time Spent Talking:** Aim for a balanced conversation where both parties get roughly equal time to speak.

Real-Life Examples of Conversational Missteps

Mike, the Interrupter

Imagine you have a friend named Mike. You're in the middle of sharing this absolutely hilarious gaming experience with the rest of your friends. The room is echoing with laughter as you start recounting the epic moment when your in-game character pulled off an unbelievable stunt, leaving everyone in stitches.

However, whenever you begin talking, Mike jumps in with his own stories, cutting you off. It's annoying, and it feels like he's not really listening. Just as you're about to deliver the punchline of your gaming triumph, Mike enthusiastically interjects, "Wait, you won't believe what happened to me last night!" You feel irritated and wonder if you'll ever get to finish telling your story.

Clio, the Conversation Controller

Imagine hanging out at the mall with your friends, where Clio, with her bold personality, takes center stage as the Conversation Controller. Eager to share your latest obsessions, you find it challenging as Clio dominates the conversation, narrating her weekend adventures non-stop. While her stories are undoubtedly interesting, it leaves little room for others to contribute to the discussion.

Clio's enthusiastic storytelling becomes a focal point, overshadowing your attempts to share your latest interests with the group. Her boldness in taking over the conversation creates an environment where others struggle to find openings to participate. The excitement of discussing your own passions at the mall takes a backseat as Clio's weekend escapades become the main event, making you wonder if there's a chance for everyone to engage in the conversation.

In both situations, these conversational missteps—*interrupting* and *dominating*—make it harder for everyone to connect and share their thoughts. It's a reminder that good communication means not just talking but also giving space for everyone's voices.

Conversation Checklist

To help avoid these common pitfalls, here's a checklist for self-evaluation:

- Did I listen more than I spoke?

- Was I mindful of not interrupting the other person?

- Did I maintain positive body language?

- Did I balance sharing personal information appropriately?

- Was I attentive to the other person's comfort level and reactions?

By being aware of these common mistakes and actively working to avoid them, conversations can transform into meaningful exchanges. Each interaction is an opportunity to practice and improve. You'll get better and better, ensuring a smooth transition from one topic to another and keeping the dialogue engaging and dynamic.

Now that we've gained insights into steering clear of conversation pitfalls, we're prepared to delve into the number one key to a great conversation: *empathy*.

EMBRACING EMPATHY

The Power of Empathy in Conversation

Meaningful conversations are centered around empathy, which is all about understanding someone else's perspective. Empathetic listening involves genuinely hearing what the other person is saying, both in words and emotions. You are stepping into their shoes, even if for one moment.

Empathy transforms conversations from mere exchanges of words to deeper connections. It's not just about understanding the other person's words but also their feelings, thoughts, and experiences. This doesn't mean you must agree with everything they say; instead, you understand where they're coming from.

Incorporating empathy into conversations involves a few essential practices:

- **Respect Different Views Without Judgment:** Be open to different points of view. Acknowledge the speaker's unique perspective and experiences without forming judgments in your mind.

- **Show You Care:** True empathy goes beyond words. Offer support or express a willingness to help when someone is facing challenges.

- **Acknowledge Their Feelings:** Recognize the emotions behind the words. A simple *"That sounds really challenging"* can go a long way.

Empathy is not only a skill — it's a gift. It allows us to connect with others on a deeper level, building stronger and more meaningful relationships. By learning to communicate with empathy, we overcome barriers and enrich our interactions, making every conversation count.

As we continue to explore the nuances of communication, the upcoming sections will explore practical exercises and techniques to enhance these skills. Becoming an expert communicator is an ongoing journey; each step brings us closer to deeper, more fulfilling connections.

THE ART OF LISTENING

When it comes to conversations, listening holds as much power as speaking, if not more. Listening is the silent half of the dialogue that turns an ordinary exchange into a meaningful interaction. This section explores the art of listening, a skill essential for anyone aiming to excel in communication.

Active listening is more than just hearing words; it's about really tuning in and connecting with what someone is saying. Being a good listener means giving your full attention, showing that you're interested, and responding in a way that lets the other person know you get where they're coming from. It's not just a useful communication skill; it can help sort out problems and strengthen your connections with others. So, next time you chat with someone, try giving them your full attention and letting them know you're on the same wavelength—it can make a big difference.

Ready to give it a go? Give these techniques a shot.

Techniques for Active Listening

- **Paraphrasing:** *Paraphrasing* involves summarizing the big picture of what someone is saying by putting it in your own words. When you paraphrase, you ensure that you've understood the speaker and show them you're listening. For example, if your friend says, *"I've had enough of the constant drama in our group, you know?"* You could say, *"So, what you're saying is, you're totally done with all the fighting going on with our friends, right?"*

- **Staying in the Moment:** Being in the moment means bringing your mind back to the conversation over and over again. Our minds like to wander – it's what humans do. Start by cutting out distractions like your phone. Even if you're listening, having your phone around sends the message that you're not entirely focused. Set yourself up for good active listening by eliminating potential interruptions and giving the person your complete attention.

- **Ask Questions:** A key way to stay engaged is by asking questions. It could be reflecting on what someone said to make sure you get it, asking them to explain more about something, or finding out how they feel about what they're talking about. When you ask questions, you show the other person that you're not just hearing them but really understanding. More on this in the following section.

- **Forget About Your Response:** Many people struggle to stay in the moment because they're too busy thinking about what to say next. Being a good listener means letting go of the pressure to come up with some life-changing reply. If you're focused on what you're going to say, you're not really listening. This part can be tricky, especially because thinking about your response is often linked to feeling anxious. But if you can quiet that inner voice, it tells the other person that you're open to learning, not just showing off what you already know.

Good listening can be a game-changer in various aspects of life. In personal relationships, active listening fosters deeper connections and trust. In conflicts, it can be the key to finding common ground and resolving issues. By truly listening, you show empathy and respect, which can transform interactions and build stronger bonds.

The Legend of Mr. Noodleman

I can't forget the incredible impact my high school Biology teacher, Mr. Noodleman, had on me. When I was stressed over the final exam and felt like no one was getting what I was going through, I decided to swing by Mr. Noodleman's office during his office hours.

I was half-expecting generic advice like "Pay more attention in class." or "You need a tutor." but Mr. Noodleman surprised me. He tuned in, leaning in, nodding, and listening without judging. He summarized my worries to show that he heard me and got where I was coming from.

This extraordinary teacher made me feel respected, heard, and cared for. He offered support and told me he was there whenever I needed help. By the end of our chat, I was tearing up with relief because no one had ever given me that kind of time, love, and attention before.

Mr. Noodleman's focus went beyond just grades; he understood the challenges of high school life. Feeling comforted and understood in that moment showed me how much he truly cared, and it stuck with me.

Reflecting on my encounter with this amazing teacher, it's clear how important *empathy, active listening,* and honing *conversation skills* can be for impacting one's life.

As we explore further, remember that the art of listening is a journey, not a destination. It's a skill that can continually be refined and improved. By practicing active listening, you're becoming not just a better communicator but also a better friend, student, and person. In the upcoming sections, we'll take a look at the more nuanced aspects of communication, building on the foundation of questioning, body language, and first impressions.

THE ART OF OPEN-ENDED QUESTIONS

Conversations are not only about sharing stories or facts; they are about asking questions that open new avenues of dialogue. Mastering the art of questioning, especially open-ended questions, is a skill that enhances the depth and quality of conversations. The key is finding a balance between asking and listening so it doesn't sound like you're just throwing questions at the other person. There's an art in using this technique, which creates space for meaningful exchanges of ideas.

The beauty in open-ended questions is that they cannot be answered with a simple *"yes"* or *"no."* They require a more detailed response and encourage others to share their thoughts and feelings. These types of questions are the key to unlocking engaging and deeper conversations.

Framing Your Questions

The secret to creating effective open-ended questions lies in how you frame them. Begin your questions with *"what," "how," "why,"* or *"tell me about…"* Instead of asking, "Did you like the movie?" try asking, "What did you think about the movie?" This encourages a more detailed response and opens the door to a richer conversation.

Timing and Appropriateness

Knowing *when* to ask a question is equally as important as knowing *what* to ask. The timing of your questions should flow naturally within the conversation. You must sense the right moment to explore deeper or shift the topic. If your friend enthusiastically tells you about a recent trip, wait for the right moment to ask, "What was the most surprising part?" Timing comes with practice, so don't worry—it will become more intuitive as you have more and more conversations.

Being sensitive to the context and mood of the conversation is also important. If the other person seems hesitant or uncomfortable, it may not be the right time to probe further. Respect their boundaries and steer the conversation to a lighter topic.

Guiding Conversations

Asking the right question at the right time can gently steer the direction of the conversation. It's like being at the helm of a ship, navigating through the waters of dialogue. Open-ended questions can uncover shared interests or opinions, creating a connected and engaging conversation.

When you discover a shared interest through your questions, it's like hitting the jackpot! This common ground makes the conversation more enjoyable and helps build a rapport with the other person. For example, finding out that you both enjoy a particular sport or hobby can take the conversation to a new level of enthusiasm and engagement.

Practice Makes Perfect

Let's look at how open-ended questioning might play out in real life. Let's say you have a love for photography. You are sitting next to someone at lunch who also enjoys photography. Instead of panicking over what to say, you use the techniques you just learned to frame your questions and steer the conversation into a meaningful and engaging open dialogue.

You: *I heard you attended that photography workshop last weekend. How did it go?*

Them: *Oh, it was fantastic! I learned some new techniques and got to experiment with different styles.*

You: *That's awesome! What techniques did you find most useful?*

Them: *Well, they taught us about capturing long exposure shots, and I never realized how fascinating and creative it could be.*

You: *Long exposure shots can produce some really cool effects. Did you have a favorite subject or scene that you tried the new techniques on?*

Them*: Absolutely. There was this old bridge near the workshop venue, and I spent a lot of time experimenting with long exposure shots of the water flowing underneath.*

You*: Nice choice! Bridges can give such amazing views, right? What was it about the flowing water that caught your attention?*

Them*: It was the play of light and shadows on the water that made it captivating. The long exposure created this beautiful, almost dreamlike effect.*

You*: Sounds magical! It seems like you had a blast at the workshop.*

Do you see how this conversation flowed? There's no better way to improve your conversation skills than to practice open-ended questioning in the real world. Here are some ways you can build on your skills.

- **Practice With Different People:** Schedule time daily to ask someone an open-ended question. They could be a family member, a friend, or a classmate. Notice how these questions change the nature of your conversations.

- **Practice In Different Settings:** Try asking open-ended questions in different settings, such as a group, one-on-one conversation, or a formal classroom setting. This process will help you understand how questioning techniques vary depending on the context.

- **Reflect On Your Questions:** After a conversation, reflect on the questions you asked. Were they open-ended? Did they contribute to the flow of the conversation? Reflecting on your questioning techniques will help you improve.

Mastering the art of questioning is a journey that enriches your conversations and relationships. You are being curious, respectful, and attentive. As you continue to practice and refine your questioning skills, you'll find that your conversations become more meaningful and rewarding.

Next, we'll explore how to interpret and use *nonverbal cues*, adding another layer to your communication skills toolkit.

THE UNSPOKEN LANGUAGE

In conversation, our words are only one part of the story. The other half of the story is nonverbal cues, often more important than spoken language. This silent form of communication can speak volumes, often revealing our true feelings and intentions.

Understanding Nonverbal Communication

Nonverbal cues include various elements, from facial expressions and eye contact to body posture and gestures. These cues can complement, reinforce, or contradict what we say verbally. Mastering the art of nonverbal communication is fundamental for understanding and being understood in daily interactions. Let's take a look at types of nonverbal communication and how we can interpret them.

Types of Nonverbal Communication

- **Facial Expressions:** The human face is extremely expressive and can show countless emotions without saying a word. Happiness, sadness, anger, surprise — each emotion is written on our faces. Learning to read these expressions can give insight into how someone is truly feeling.

- **Eye Contact:** Eyes can convey a range of emotions and intentions. Direct eye contact can indicate interest, attention, or attraction, while a lack of eye contact might suggest discomfort or evasion. How someone looks at you or avoids your gaze can be a significant nonverbal cue.

- **Body Posture and Gestures:** How we sit, stand, and move says a lot about our attitude and emotions. Open body postures, like keeping your arms uncrossed, signal you're comfortable and at ease. On the other hand, closed postures like folded arms might mean you're feeling defensive or out of your comfort zone. Gestures play a significant role in communication, too. A nod's like saying, *"Yeah, I'm with you,"* while a shrug is a move that means, *"I'm kinda meh about it."*

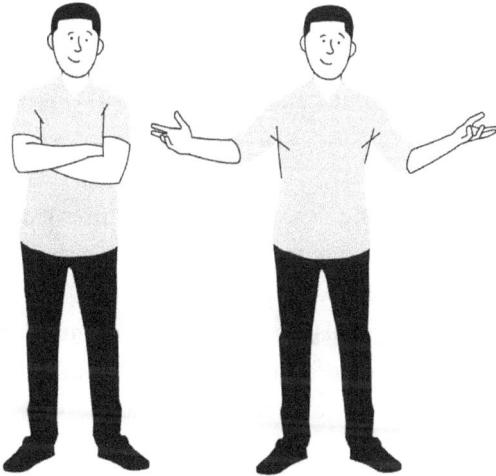

Tips for Reading Nonverbal Cues

- **Context Matters:** When reading non-verbal cues, you need to tune in to the context of the situation (what's going on) and the person (who you're dealing with). For example, what recent events or personal experiences have they been dealing with? Knowing what's going on in their lives will help you understand them tremendously.

- **Look for Trends:** A single gesture or expression might not mean much, but a series of cues can give a clearer picture. For example, if a friend always sits with their arms crossed, it could just be a comfortable position for them. However, it could mean defensiveness if that's not a trend you usually see.

- **Consider Cultural Differences:** Nonverbal communication can vary significantly across cultures. What's considered polite in one culture might be rude in another. For example, in many Western cultures, a thumbs-up is commonly used to express approval or agreement. However, in some Middle Eastern and Asian cultures, a thumbs-up can be interpreted as offensive or disrespectful.

Reading and interpreting nonverbal cues requires careful observation and sensitivity. Picking up on these cues is critical for smooth communication and connecting with others on a personal level. As you practice these skills, conversations become more nuanced, and your understanding of others will deepen. In the next section, we will focus on how to make first impressions count.

MASTERING FIRST IMPRESSIONS

When meeting new people, the first impression packs a powerful punch. It's like a quick snapshot someone takes of you in their mind within seconds of the introduction. In this chapter, we're diving into the nitty-gritty of first impressions and giving you down-to-earth advice on how to make a great one.

First impressions happen quickly and depend on factors such as how you look, carry yourself, and even sound. These snap judgments are typically made without thought, setting the stage for whatever comes next. They're a big deal because they lay the groundwork for any relationship, whether hanging out with new friends or working with new people.

Why First Impressions Matter

A solid first impression can open doors to new opportunities and relationships. It can influence how others perceive your trustworthiness, competence, and friendliness. On the other hand, a poor first impression can be challenging to reverse and may lead to missed opportunities. Making a positive first impression is not about putting on a show; it's about presenting the best, most authentic version of yourself. Here are some tips to help you do just that:

- **Appearance Matters:** Dress appropriately for the occasion. Your clothes don't need to be extravagant, but you should look neat and put together. With the proper attire, you show respect for yourself and the situation.

- **A Warm, Genuine Smile:** People commonly see a smile as a sign of friendliness. A genuine smile can make you seem approachable and open. It helps to ease any nerves between you and other people.

- **Confident Body Language:** Stand tall, make eye contact, and offer a firm handshake (where culturally appropriate) —these nonverbal cues project confidence and openness.

- **Positive and Engaging Conversation:** Start with light, positive topics. This method sets a comfortable tone for the interaction. See Chapter 4 for some wonderful ice breakers.

- **Pay Attention to Tone of Voice:** Your tone can easily give off confidence, warmth, and enthusiasm. Be mindful of not just *what* you say but *how* you say it.

Crafting a killer first impression combines a winning attitude with solid communication skills. Master first impressions and every new encounter becomes an opportunity to shine.

———

Now that we've got the fundamentals of conversation under our belt, it's time to level up our game. In the upcoming chapter, I will show you how to take that terrifying first step, walk up to someone, and initiate a conversation. Don't worry; I will give you tons of icebreakers and conversation starters, so you know exactly what to say. And after connecting with someone, I will show you how to turn those brief interactions into lasting friendships.

CHAPTER 4
INITIATE INTERACTIONS
(I)

> "You can make more friends in two months by becoming interested in other people than you can in two years by trying to get other people interested in you." — Dale Carnegie

This iconic quote encapsulates the core of our exploration in this chapter: *initiating meaningful conversations.*

Let's be real; we've all been in that position where you see someone you'd love to chat with, but you're stuck on how to kick things off. As Dale Carnegie suggests, the secret is being genuinely interested in the other person. So, if you're ever wondering how to break the ice, just remember, it's all about showing some real curiosity and making those connections.

Initiating interactions with other people is like jumping into a pool. It can seem scary at first, but once you're in and you've wiped the cold water out of your eyes, you realize how much fun it can be. And you know the best part? You're about to become a pro at starting conversations. This chapter isn't just about talking to others; it's about making people feel at ease around you. Creating that positive atmosphere is the secret to starting and building lasting relationships.

First things first, let's talk about breaking the ice. Do you ever feel stumped about what to say after the initial "*hi*?" We've *all* been there. The secret is finding those perfect icebreakers that don't feel forced. And guess what? They're easier to find than you might think. We will explore different ways to start conversations that feel natural and leave a lasting impression.

But how about online chats? I've got you covered there too. Starting conversations on social media or text messaging can be a whole different ball game. You'll get tips on crafting messages that grab attention without getting lost in the sea of DMs.

Keep in mind, it's not just about starting a chat; it's about keeping it going. You'll discover how to turn small talk into meaningful conversations that make the other person want to continue talking with you. These skills include follow-up questions, showing genuine interest, and finding common ground.

HOW TO APPROACH PEOPLE

Walking up to someone new and starting a conversation can feel like the hardest thing in the world. But here's the deal: it's the most crucial step in forming friendships. Why? Because every friendship starts with a simple "*Hello*."

Many of us get nervous about talking to someone new. Some thoughts running through your mind might sound like, "*I'm going to blow this whole thing*," or "*They're going to think I'm an idiot!*" These fears are typical but not always true. Most people are happy to chat and just as eager to make a new friend as you.

So, how do you approach someone for the first time? It's easier than you might think. Here are some simple steps to follow:

1. Find the Right Moment: Look for a time when the person isn't busy or rushing around. This moment could be during lunch at school, a community event, or in a line at a store.

. . .

2. Start with a Smile: A warm smile is a universal sign of friendliness. It shows you're approachable and kind.

3. **Use a Simple Greeting:** Start with a basic "Hi, I'm [your name]" or "Hey, what's up." It's simple but effective.

4. **Listen Actively:** When they reply, show you're listening. Nod your head, make eye contact, and respond to their words. This shows you're genuinely interested in the conversation.

5. **Share a Little About Yourself:** Don't share too much upfront; leave room for the conversation to continue. For example you could say something like, "I'm really into music, especially playing the guitar."

6. **Be Open to Their Response:** They might share something about themselves — this is a good sign. It means they're interested in talking to you.

Here's an example dialogue to give you an idea:

You: "*Hey, I saw you in the science lab. You seemed really into the experiment. What do you think of Mrs. Thompson?* "

Them: "*She's the nicest teacher. I'm thinking about joining the science club.*"

You: "*That's cool. I've been thinking about joining, too. Maybe we could go check it out together?*"

Them: "*Sure, that sounds great!*"

Do you see how naturally the conversation flowed? You need to search for common ground and show interest in the other person. Remember, the goal isn't to impress them; it's to start a genuine connection.

Now, it's important to note that not every attempt will lead to a long conversation or a new friendship — that's okay. The more you practice, the better you'll get at the initiation process. Plus, each time you try, you get braver and improve your social skills.

So, the next time you see someone you want to talk to, take a deep breath and go for it. Something as simple as saying "*hi*" can open the door to a new friendship. Remember, everyone's a little nervous about making the first move. But once you do, you'll find that most people are just waiting for someone to talk to them. Who knows, the next person you approach could end up being your best friend.

ICEBREAKERS - MORE THAN JUST WORDS

In social situations, whether a party, a new class at school, or even a casual meet-up, starting a conversation can sometimes feel unnatural or forced. This is where icebreakers come in. Icebreakers are fun questions that ease the tension, spark interest, and get the conversation flowing to make everyone feel more at home.

It might feel uncomfortable when you first start using icebreaker questions. To alleviate these awkward feelings, start by saying something like, *"Okay, here's a fun icebreaker for you."* before beginning.

Here are some icebreakers that you can use in different settings:

At Parties:

- *"If you could have dinner with any fictional character, who would it be and why?"* — This question opens a world of possibilities and fun responses. It's a great way to learn about someone's interests and tastes in a light-hearted way.

- *"What's the most binge-worthy show you've watched recently, and what made it so captivating?"* — TV shows often provide a common ground for many people; this question can lead to a lively discussion about shared interests.

In School:

- *"If you could pick a subject that isn't taught in school but should be, what would it be?"* — This question can lead to creative and unexpected answers, giving insight into the other person's interests and thoughts about education.

- *"Who's been your favorite teacher this school year, and what makes them great?"* — *Asking about a favorite teacher can open up positive conversations and help discover shared experiences and feelings about school life.*

General Icebreakers:

- *"What's a hobby you've always wanted to try but haven't yet?"* — This question is great for uncovering hidden desires and can lead to conversations about dreams and aspirations.

- *"If you had a superpower for a day, what would it be and why?"* — A fun and imaginative question that can lead to a playful and engaging conversation.

Tips For Using Icebreakers

Remember, icebreakers are just a way to get the conversation flowing. They show the other person you're interested in chatting and allow them to share something about themselves. The best icebreakers are those that feel natural and relevant to the situation.

When using icebreakers, be genuine and attentive. Listen to their answers and respond with interest. This allows you to discover shared hobbies, experiences, and views.

As you use these icebreakers, you'll find that starting conversations becomes easier and more enjoyable. Each interaction is a chance to learn something new, not just about others but also about yourself. With each conversation, you're building the skills and confidence needed to succeed in social situations.

Go ahead and use these icebreakers; watch as conversations flow and new connections form. Remember, every great friendship starts with a simple exchange of words. Let these icebreakers be your guide to a world of exciting social interactions. Let's make those first words count!

DIGITAL ICEBREAKERS: HOW TO START CONVERSATIONS ONLINE

In the digital world, starting a conversation can be as tricky as navigating a new app for the first time. With their screens and keyboards, online platforms create a whole new landscape for social interactions. The core principles of starting a conversation remain the same: be genuine, be respectful, and be engaging.

The Art of the Online Introduction

In the online world, you can't rely on body language or tone of voice; your words need to do the heavy lifting. Here's how to make them count:

- **Be Personal, But Not Too Personal:** Start with something specific to their profile or post. For example, "*I saw your post about hiking. The view looked amazing! I love hiking, too. Do you have any trail recommendations?*" — This specific message shows you've taken the time to understand their interests.

- **Keep the Chat Flowing:** Toss in questions that make online chatting easy going and fun. Instead of just asking,

"Did you enjoy your trip?" try asking, *"What was the best part of your hiking trip?"* — This technique allows for more engaging responses and a deeper conversation.

- **Share a Bit About Yourself:** For instance, *"Last summer, I explored this amazing trail with amazing views. Ever stumbled upon a hidden gem while hiking? I'd love to hear about your favorite trails or memorable hiking stories!"* This way, you're fostering a two-way street for the conversation.

Navigating the Nuances of Online Communication

Without the benefit of physical reactions, we can often misinterpret online messages. Here's how to navigate these waters:

- **Keep It Light:** Humor goes a long way, but remember that it's hard to convey tone online. Stick to light, friendly jokes that won't be misunderstood.

- **Emojis and Exclamation Points:** These can help convey tone and enthusiasm. A smiley face or a laughing emoji can make your intent clear and your message friendlier.

- **Patience Is Key:** People may not respond immediately online. Unlike face-to-face interactions, online conversations can span hours or even days. Patience shows respect for their time and schedule.

The Difference Between Digital and In-Person Conversation

Chatting with someone online isn't quite like talking face-to-face. You miss out on all those tiny details you get when hanging out in person. When you're face-to-face, you can pick up on cues like tone, facial expressions, and body language. But on the internet, you've got to figure out what someone means just from their words. It doesn't mean online chats are less important — they're just a bit different.

Your words need to be well thought out and clear. Things can get misconstrued easily when you can't see the other person's reactions. Always be transparent about your intentions and feelings.

Strategies for Engaging Online Conversations

- **Stay Current:** Bring up a recent event or trend. *"Have you tried that new game everyone's talking about?"* Talking about the newest trends will show you're in tune with what's happening around you.

- **Find Shared Interests:** Just like in real life, shared interests are a great foundation for conversation. Join groups or forums based on your interests and start conversations.

- **Respect Boundaries:** Remember, everyone has different comfort levels online. If someone doesn't seem interested in chatting, don't worry. There are plenty of other people to connect with.

Digital icebreakers open the door to new friendships and connections. The key lies in being genuine, respectful, and engaging. With these tips, you're all set to navigate the online social landscape with confidence. Remember, behind every screen is a person looking to share and connect with others. So go ahead and send that message; watch as your digital world expands with new friends and conversations.

Capturing Attention: Say Something Worth Remembering

The first words in any conversation are like the headline of a newspaper article; they can either grab someone's attention or be easily forgotten. In social situations, a compelling opening line or question sparks interest and engages others in meaningful dialogue.

The Power of a Great Opening

Why is the opening so important? Because it sets the tone for the rest of the conversation. A great opening can intrigue, amuse, or provoke thought, leading to a deeper and more enjoyable interaction. It's your chance to show that you're interesting, thoughtful, and worth spending time with.

Crafting Engaging Conversation Starters

So, how do you come up with these engaging conversation starters? Expand your horizons beyond the typical *"What do you do?"* or *"Nice weather, isn't it?"* Start by talking about what's happening around you and asking questions specific to the person or your surroundings. Unlike icebreakers, which are fun and often unrelated questions, conversation starters are specific to your environment. Here are some ideas:

- *"I noticed your vintage camera strap. That's pretty cool. What's the story behind it?"* — This shows you're paying attention and can lead to a personal yet casual conversation.

- *"I love this song! I've been trying to find some new music lately. Got any recommendations?"* — If you're both into music, this can be a great way to bond over shared tastes or discover new tunes.

- *"I'm starving. What's your go-to place for food around here?"* — This opening line is perfect if you're at a school event or in a new place. It's casual and might lead to discovering common favorite spots or foods.

- *"How long have you been into [a hobby or activity they are doing or talking about]?"* — This question shows you're interested in what they're into and can lead to a deeper conversation about passions and hobbies.

Using these kinds of opening lines shows that you're not just making small talk; you're interested in a genuine conversation. They invite people to share something personal and meaningful, setting the stage for a deeper connection.

Remember, the goal is to start a conversation and engage in an interesting and meaningful exchange. Your opening line is your first impression in a conversation, so make it count. A well-chosen question or comment can turn a routine interaction into a memorable one. Next time you find yourself in a social setting, try one of these conversation starters. You might be surprised at how much more engaging and enjoyable your conversations become.

CONTEXT MATTERS

The setting in which you are trying to make friends or start a conversation can change the rules of the game. Mastering the art of conversation in various social settings is like being a DJ at a party; you need to play the right tune for the right crowd. Here are some tips to adjust your conversation starters, or icebreakers, to fit different environments:

At Parties:

Parties are fun, relaxed, and usually full of people ready to mingle — conversations are light and casual. What is your approach, you may ask? Be yourself and be prepared to join in on the fun. You might start a conversation by commenting on the music, the decorations, or even the food. "This pizza is amazing, isn't it?" Little remarks like these are simple but effective in opening doors to further conversation.

Community Gatherings:

Community events are a mixed bag. They can be casual, like a party, but they often have a purpose. The key is to find a balance. You might start a conversation based on the event's theme. At a local fundraiser, you could say, *"It's great to see the community coming together for a good cause, don't you think?"* These kinds of chats show that you're engaged with the community and creates opportunity for diverse conversations.

. . .

At School or College:

In educational settings where people share everyday experiences, start with something related to school life. For example, *"What do you think of Mrs. Smith's surprise quizzes?"* or *"Have you decided on your project topic for science class?"* This initiates a conversation and shows you're both in the same boat.

Real-Life Examples:

- **Party Scenario:** Max notices someone standing alone at a friend's birthday party. He walks over with a smile and asks, *"So, how do you know the birthday boy?"* This shared link provides a comfortable starting point for the conversation.

- **Community Scenario:** At a neighborhood block party, Mia and Jordan notice the lively atmosphere. Mia points to the vibrant decorations, saying, "These decorations really add a festive touch to the party, don't you think?" Jordan smiles and agrees. By casually starting a chat about the block party's theme, Mia sets the stage for connecting with a potential new friend.

- **School Scenario:** Ava sees a new student, Jayden, looking lost in the hallway. She approaches him and says, *"Hey, the school layout is pretty confusing at first, isn't it? Need help finding your next class?"* This simple gesture of help not only breaks the ice but also offers a helping hand.

In these scenarios, the key is choosing a conversation starter that suits the setting and feels natural. These conversation starters make the other person comfortable and pave the way for a more engaging and rewarding chat.

Each setting demands a slightly different version of you. At a party, you're the fun-loving individual. And at community gatherings, you're the engaged community member, contributing your ideas and actively participating in discussions. Understanding these nuances can make all the difference in how you're perceived and how you connect with others.

The magic of mastering context lies in observing and adapting. Pay attention to the mood, the people, and the overall vibe of the place. This observation will give you clues about how to approach conversations and what topics to discuss. Being adaptable doesn't mean changing who you are; it's about adjusting how you present yourself in different situations. So, next time you find yourself in a social setting, take a moment to read the room and dive in.

THE FOLLOW-UP: MAKING IT LAST

After breaking the ice and starting a conversation, the real magic lies in keeping it going and turning it into a lasting connection. This part is fundamental because it's where relationships are built and strengthened.

The Role of Follow-Up Questions

Follow-up questions are your best tools for keeping a conversation alive. They show you're interested and paying attention. More importantly, they allow the other person to express themselves sincerely, which is key to forming connections. For example, if someone mentions they play guitar, follow up with, "*What got you started with guitar?*" or "*What's your favorite song to play?*"

Tips for Keeping the Conversation Flowing

- **Wait to Respond:** This is a skill that takes practice, especially when you have a lot to share. Take time to *really* hear what the other person is saying, don't just wait for your turn to speak. Nod, make eye contact, and respond to what they've said before adding your own thoughts.

- **Balance Sharing and Asking:** Make sure you're not just talking about yourself. Share a bit, then turn the focus back to the other person. This balance creates a back-and-forth flow that feels natural and engaging.

- **Discover Shared Interests:** If you find common ground, dive into it. Shared passions can serve as the basis for building strong connections.

- **Be Curious:** Show genuine interest in what they're saying. Ask questions that encourage them to share more about their experiences and opinions. Channeling Dale Carnegie's wisdom, remember that showing genuine interest in others can create stronger connections and make conversations more engaging and meaningful.

- **Use Humor Wisely:** A well-timed joke or funny comment can lighten the mood; make sure it's appropriate and doesn't make the other person uncomfortable.

Turning Brief Interactions into Lasting Connections

Transforming short conversations into lasting connections involves more than just talking; it's about forming meaningful bonds. Here are some strategies:

- **Follow-Up After the Conversation:** If you've exchanged contact information, send a text referencing something you discussed. For instance, "*I saw this article about guitar-*

playing techniques and thought of our conversation. Thought you might find it interesting."

- **Plan Future Interactions:** If you both enjoyed the conversation, suggest another meet-up. *"We should totally meet up for a coffee next week! Are you around after school?"*

- **Show Consistent Interest:** In future interactions, bring up things they've mentioned before, such as, *"How's your guitar practice going?"* This attention to detail shows you remember and care about their interests.

- **Be Supportive:** If they share a challenge they're facing, offer your support or help. You could say something like, *"Hey, if you ever need someone to talk to about the challenges you're facing, I'm here for you."* This support can deepen the trust and bond between you.

- **Remember Names:** People appreciate when you remember their names. Using a person's name while chatting with them adds a personal touch to your interactions. Saying, *"Ok, Adam, it was so nice talking to you."* shows that you took the time to remember them, making the conversation more personal and meaningful.

Every great friendship or relationship starts with a simple conversation. By using these strategies, you can turn brief interactions into lasting friendships. Keep the conversation going, show genuine interest, and before you know it, you'll have turned a new acquaintance into a friend.

———

Okay, so you've mastered the art of initiating conversations. But what comes next? How do you turn these fresh connections into meaningful, lasting friendships? In the next chapter, we'll explore the journey from the initial greeting to a deep and lasting bond.

Chapter 5 focuses on continuing to build on the foundations we have established. Starting a conversation is only surface level; creating friendships from that initial spark is another level. We'll explore the nuances of deepening these new connections and understanding the subtle art of nurturing and growing a relationship.

So, if you're ready to move beyond the first step and create friendships that stand the test of time, stay with me. The next chapter is your guide to transforming brief interactions into friendships that enrich your life and bring joy, support, and a sense of belonging.

CHAPTER 5
ASSEMBLE AUTHENTIC FRIENDSHIPS (A)

> "True friendship comes when the silence between two people is comfortable." - David Tyson

Think about this for a moment. When you're with a good friend, can you just sit there, not saying anything at all, and still feel totally okay? That's the sign of a real, solid friendship. It's like having a comfortable pair of sneakers; they fit just right, no matter where you go.

In this chapter, we're diving into the world of true friendships. You know, the kind where someone's got your back, no matter what. We're not just talking about people you hang out with. We're talking about friends who are like your personal cheer squad, who help you pick up the pieces on a bad day, and who can laugh with you until your stomach hurts.

True friends see and love the real you. They're the ones who appreciate your weird obsession with collecting stickers or your fear of clowns and yet they still stick around. These unique quirks become shared jokes and stories, making every moment together special and filled with laughter.

Now, you may be wondering, where do you find these mythical *good friends?* They're not hiding under rocks or in secret clubs — they're all around you. They could be the person sitting next to you in class, someone from your soccer team, or someone you bump into at the library. The trick is to be open to making new connections and recognizing the signs of a genuine friendship prospect.

So, get ready to explore the craft of making and keeping authentic friendships. It's a journey that's totally worth it, filled with laughter, learning, and lots of memorable moments. Let's get started.

QUALITIES OF A GOOD FRIEND

What exactly makes someone a good friend? It's a question that might seem simple at first; however, the answer is as unique as each friendship. Everyone has their own idea of what a true friend should be like. Let's unravel this question together and explore the qualities of genuine friendships.

First off, a good friend is someone who's *loyal*. Imagine having someone always in your corner, whether acing a school project or fumbling through a bad day. Loyalty isn't about being physically present all the time; it's knowing this person won't ditch you when things get tough. It's a silent promise, a commitment to stick by you.

Second, a good friend prioritizes *honesty*. It's easy to tell someone what they *want* to hear, but a real friend tells you what you *need* to hear. It's like when they gently point out that your crush might not be the best choice, not to be harsh, but because they care about your feelings and want what's best for you.

What about being *reliable?* A good friend is someone you can count on. They're the ones you call when you need help, like when you're stuck with a flat tire at midnight, and they show up without hesitation. Reliability means being the same awesome person today, tomorrow, and the day after.

Supportiveness is critical, too. Friends lift each other up, celebrating victories and offering a shoulder to lean on during defeats. Being there for your friends does not have to be a grand gesture. The small, everyday actions you do for each other show you care.

Now, how about a *sense of humor?* Life's full of ups and downs; sometimes, what you need most is a good laugh. A friend who can crack a joke to lighten the mood or laugh at themselves is a ray of sunshine on a cloudy day.

And then there's the quality of being *nonjudgmental.* Good friends accept you for who you are. They don't try to change you or judge your choices. Friends understand that everyone makes mistakes, and these mistakes don't define you.

(Note: If I ever find myself becoming judgmental of my friends, I often remind myself with a simple mantra: "*These are your friends; love it or leave it.*" It's a cue to resist judgmental thoughts and remember that nobody is perfect, and we *all* have flaws.)

Finally, a good friend is *respectful.* They value your opinions and feelings, even if they differ from their own. This respect allows friendships to thrive amidst differences and disagreements.

Good Friend Checklist

Consider this checklist to assess the qualities you possess in friendships:

- **Loyalty**: Are you there for your friends when they need you?

- **Honesty**: Do you share your genuine thoughts in a kind and helpful way?

- **Supportiveness**: Do you celebrate your friends' successes and support them in tough times?

- **Sense of Humor:** Can you bring a smile to your friends faces?

- **Nonjudgmental**: Do you accept your friends as they are, without trying to change them?

- **Respect**: Do you value and consider your friends' feelings and opinions?

These qualities are ingredients for building solid and lasting friendships. They transform acquaintances into true friends, the kind that last a lifetime. Each friendship is a unique blend of these qualities, creating a bond that's special in its own way. It's not about finding perfect friends but about finding those perfect for you.

Friendships in Real-Time

During my teen years, my best friend Lauren was not just a friend but a beacon of support for me. When I received that hard-earned A on my biology final in Mr. Noodleman's class, Lauren went beyond mere congratulations; she genuinely celebrated my success, adding to the joy with her infectious enthusiasm. The following day, she surprised me by hanging colorful decorations and cards inside my locker to show how happy she was for me. That's a *supportive* friend.

Lauren was also there for me when I had my first breakup. She didn't offer clichéd advice or try to fix everything; instead, she was just *there*. She let me come over after school and lounge on her couch--giving me that comforting space where I could openly express my feelings. She was understanding and willing to be there for me—she didn't say *"I told you so"* or try to set me up with someone else. She was my *loyal* rock.

Lauren wasn't just a friend; she was a steadfast pillar of support. Whether celebrating my victories with infectious enthusiasm or providing a comforting haven during heartbreaks without clichéd advice, Lauren exemplified the essence of a true and supportive friend. As we delve into the next section, let's explore exactly how to find the perfect friend.

HOW TO FIND A GOOD FRIEND

Finding a good friend is like discovering a hidden gem. It's not always easy, and sometimes you have to dig through a lot of dirt to find that one sparkly stone. But when you do, it's worth every bit of effort. So, where do you start your search for these gems, especially as a teenager? Let's unfold this treasure map together.

The hunt for good friends often begins in familiar territories: your school, neighborhood, or local hangouts. You spend a lot of time in these places, making them ideal for stumbling upon potential friends. In school, look beyond your immediate classroom. There may be someone in your art class who catches your eye with their creative projects or someone in the library who shares your love for mystery novels. Keep your eyes open and notice those around you.

Activities and clubs are a goldmine for meeting like-minded people. Whether it's sports, music, drama, or a tech club, these groups bring together people with similar interests. Real connections are made through finding someone who shares your passions, not just your hobbies.

But how do you know if someone could be a good friend? Look out for small signs. A potential friend is someone who listens to you, shows genuine interest in your thoughts and feelings, and respects your opinions, even if they differ from yours. They're the ones who make you feel comfortable being yourself, who laugh at your jokes, and who offer a helping hand without being asked.

Another sign of a potential good friend is how they treat others. Are they kind and respectful to everyone, not just you? This kindness is a sign of a genuinely nice person who will likely be a good friend.

Shared interests and values are the cornerstone of lasting friendships. It's great to have a friend who loves the same band as you, but it's even better when they share your values: honesty, kindness, or hard work. These shared values create a deeper connection, one that goes beyond just having fun together.

BUILDING TRUST IN FRIENDSHIPS

Trust is the foundation of every good friendship. It's the invisible thread that ties two people together, letting them know that they can rely on each other. Without trust, friendships are like houses built on sand – shaky and ready to collapse at the first sign of trouble.

What is trust, and why is it so important in friendships? Trust means knowing that your friend will do what they say they will do. It means believing they will keep your secrets, support you, and not purposely hurt you. It means feeling safe, secure, and at home with this person.

Building trust grows slowly like a plant, sprouting from seeds of small actions and words. Here's how you can nurture this growth:

- **Be Reliable:** If you say you will do something, do it. Whether returning a borrowed book or keeping a promise, these actions speak louder than words.

- **Speak Your Heart:** Share your thoughts and feelings openly with your friend. Don't keep things bottled up inside. This openness will reinforce trust in your relationship.

- **Keep Secrets:** If a friend confides in you, guard that secret like a treasure. Breaking confidentiality is one of the fastest ways to break trust.

Just as there are ways to build trust, actions can also break it. Here are a few to be mindful of:

- **Gossiping:** Talking behind a friend's back is a surefire way to break trust; spreading rumors can cause irreparable damage.

- **Lying:** Even small lies can fracture trust. Little fibs might seem harmless, but honesty is the glue that holds trust together, so it's best to keep it real with your friends.

- **Ignoring Boundaries:** Pushing a friend's limits or disregarding their comfort can significantly damage trust. If a friend is not comfortable doing something, respect their boundaries.

- **Being Unsupportive**: If you're not there for your friend when they need you, they might start to question your commitment. Being a reliable friend in both good and tough times is essential; not showing up when your friend needs you most can erode the trust they have in you.

Breaking Trust in Real-Time

You have a best friend named Hannah. Excitedly sharing her crush on Jake, Hannah asks you to keep it a secret. You, agreeing solemnly, assure her that her secret is safe.

A week later, the high school rumor mill is buzzing with news of Hannah's crush on Jake. Shocked and hurt, Hannah confronted you, only to discover that you had shared her secret with a few others, thinking it wouldn't spread far. The damage was done, and your once-unbreakable trust was now strained.

This scenario illustrates how seemingly innocent actions, like sharing a secret with a select few, can lead to significant consequences. The fallout left Hannah feeling betrayed, emphasizing the importance of respecting trust in friendships.

It serves as a reminder that trust is delicate. Once broken, it's hard to repair. But with care, respect, and consistency, you can build a bond of trust that will make your friendships stronger and more meaningful. As you move through your friendships, keep these points in mind. They will guide you in forming connections that are fun, fulfilling, and deeply rooted in this foundation of trust.

BEING AUTHENTIC

In Chapter 1, we explored the concept of authenticity and how it relates to self-awareness. Authenticity is all about being true to yourself and keeping it real in your interactions and relationships. When you are authentic, you can express your true thoughts, feelings, and identity without pretense or needing approval.

When I was in high school, what I wanted more than anything was to be accepted and to fit in. So, to blend in with everyone else, I pretended to be a massive fan of the popular 90s TV show *Dawson's Creek*. Everyone was always talking about it, but the truth was, I never saw a single episode of the show. Maintaining the facade became exhausting, and the fear of exposure made every interaction feel like a balancing act.

The breaking point came when a classmate, a true *Dawson's Creek* enthusiast, quizzed me, exposing my lack of knowledge. It was a wake-up call — pretending strained my authenticity and made me look like a phony.

After that humiliating moment, I realized it's far better to come clean as an authentic person (who didn't actually like the show) than to stand out as someone who fakes interest just to fit in.

How do you make sure you are genuinely being authentic in your friendships? Let's take a look.

Nurturing Authentic Friendships

- **Share Your True Thoughts:** Start with something simple. Share an honest opinion about a movie or a book, even if you're the only one who liked it. Work on finding your voice and being comfortable expressing it.

- **Share Your True Interests:** Don't pretend to like something just because your friends do. Share your real hobbies and interests. It's okay if you like to knit or collect vintage action figures–your real friends will appreciate you for being you.

- **Stay True to Your Values:** If something doesn't feel right to you, like skipping class or cheating on a test, it's okay to say no. Always stick to your belief system.

- **Admit Your Mistakes:** Everyone makes mistakes from time to time. Being authentic means owning up to your mistakes and learning from them.

- **Ask For Help When You Need It:** Asking for help shows that you trust your friends and that you're human, just like them.

Sometimes, however, showing your true self can feel scary. You might worry about being judged or not fitting in. Here are some tips for those times:

- **Start Small:** Share a little at a time. You don't have to reveal everything at once. For example, I could've casually mentioned that *Dawson's Creek* wasn't my go-to show. This way, I'd be truthful without pretending to be a die-hard fan, allowing me to be genuine while navigating social dynamics.

- **Find the Right Moment:** Look for times when it feels natural to share something about yourself. For example, maybe you love to write poetry but don't want to share it right away. Whether it's during a heart-to-heart conversation or a casual hangout, choosing the right moment helps make your sharing more meaningful.

- **Choose the Right Friends:** Share your true self with friends who make you feel safe and supported. Surround yourself with those who appreciate your authenticity, creating a positive environment for genuine connections to flourish.

- **Trust the Process:** Being authentic takes practice. It's okay if it doesn't happen overnight. Embrace the journey of self-expression, knowing that with time and experience, authenticity becomes a more natural and effortless part of your friendships.

Authenticity is not just about being honest with others and yourself. It's understanding who you are and being brave enough to show that person to the world. Authentic friendships are built on truth and openness. These friendships last long, have value, and bring absolute joy and connection.

MAINTAINING FRIENDSHIPS FOR THE LONG HAUL

You and your best friend, Hannah, are facing the challenge of attending different colleges in different cities. This introduces a bit of distance that could potentially put a strain on your long-term friendship. Despite the physical separation, you decide to navigate this new chapter by setting up weekly video chats, attempting to keep the lines of communication wide open.

As you both navigate through college life, changes start happening. Maybe Hannah discovers a new passion, and you get into your major, potentially leading to a sense of drifting apart.

While you grapple with these changes, the evolving nature of your lives becomes more apparent. The physical distance emphasizes the emotional gap that naturally occurs when two close friends find themselves in different places, both physically and metaphorically.

In the journey of life, friendships can be tested by many challenges. Distance, life changes, and unexpected twists can sometimes put a strain on the strongest bonds. Maintaining long-term friendships is akin to nurturing a garden; it requires care, patience, and understanding. But don't worry; with the right tools, you can transform these friendships into ones that last a lifetime.

Let's talk about some common challenges that friendships face and how to navigate through them.

Common Barriers to Long-Term Friendships

- **Distance:** When friends move away for college, work, or family reasons, the physical distance can create an emotional gap. The trick is keeping the bond strong, even when you're miles apart.

- **Life Changes:** As people grow, their lives change. Friends might get new jobs, start relationships, or develop new interests. These changes can create a feeling of drifting apart. Make sure to respect these changes and grow together.

- **Taking Each Other for Granted:** Sometimes, in long-term friendships, people start taking each other for granted. Appreciate your friends, celebrate their successes, and support them through failures. Show gratitude for their presence in your life.

- **Neglect:** In the hustle of life, friends might feel neglected. Making time for your friends is important, even when life gets busy. A simple text, a random call, or a surprise visit can go a long way in making your friends feel valued.

- **Not Sharing Feelings:** Friends often hold back from sharing their true feelings to avoid conflict. However, honest communication is key to maintaining strong friendships. Share your feelings in a respectful and understanding way.

Overcoming Long-Term Friendship Barriers

Maintaining long-term friendships is a skill. This skill requires nurturing the bond you share with care, understanding, and a little creativity. In a world where everything seems temporary, a lasting friendship is a treasure. Let's explore some practical ways to keep these friendships strong over time:

- **Regular Communication:** This is the lifeline of any friendship. In the era of technology, staying in touch has never been easier. Use messaging apps to share daily happenings, funny memes, or share a simple *"how are you?"* A quick text can go a long way in helping someone. Share updates about your life, no matter how small.

- **Scheduled Meet-Ups:** Life gets busy; however, making time for friends is essential. Plan regular meet-ups, whether a monthly coffee date, a yearly trip, or a video call. Use calendar apps to set reminders for these meet-ups.

- **Remember Important Details:** Remembering birthdays, anniversaries, or small details such as their favorite food or movie shows that you care. Use reminder apps to keep track of these important dates.

- **Forgiveness:** No one is perfect. If, for example, a friend forgot to call you back, be ready to forgive and move on past mistakes. Holding grudges only weakens the bond.

- **Embrace Technology:** Utilize social media and apps to stay connected, especially if you're in different parts of the world. Apps like Skype, Zoom, or WhatsApp can bridge the distance.

Maintaining friendships requires hard work, patience, and a lot of love — the benefits are immeasurable. Good friends can improve your mental and emotional health, provide support in tough times, and bring joy and laughter into your life.

They are your cheerleaders, advisors, and companions in the journey of life. As you grow and navigate through different phases, these friendships can be your anchor, providing a sense of belonging and stability. Keep in mind, it's not the quantity of friends that matters but the quality of the friendships you nurture. By following these strategies, you can ensure that these bonds not only survive but also flourish over the years.

Long-Term Friendships in Real-Time

Even now, I can't help but boast about my fantastic group of friends— small but rock-solid, and we've been holding it down for years. We keep our connection strong with daily memes and heartfelt texts. Our monthly coffee dates are sacred, where we catch up on life's dramas and share the latest scoop. And, of course, our annual road trip is the ultimate adventure, packed with carefully planned escapades that we spend months looking forward to.

Over the years, life's thrown us some curveballs, but we roll with the punches. New jobs, relationships, personal growth—we've faced it all, and it's only strengthened our crew.

Video calls and surprise visits? That's just our way of saying distance can't touch us. Every time we meet up, it's like adding a fresh chapter to our wild story, proving our friendships are as solid as they come. Through laughter, dreams, and endless support, our crew remains tight, turning every moment into a celebration of our shared journey.

As you can see, keeping up with your crew is totally worth it – the strong connections and epic celebrations prove that the effort pays off big time.

CONFLICT RESOLUTION

Navigating conflicts with friends is a natural part of the journey as you grow your relationships. Learning to handle conflicts maturely is a skill that not only saves friendships but also makes them stronger and more resilient. Just like any skill, you will improve with every conflict.

The first step in conflict resolution is acknowledging that disagreements are normal. No two people are the same; differences in opinions or expectations are bound to occur. It's how these conflicts are handled that makes all the difference.

Here are some techniques for effectively resolving conflicts:

- **Stay Calm and Respectful:** Even if you're upset, focus on keeping your cool. Respectful communication, without yelling or name-calling, helps keep the conversation productive.

- **Express Your Feelings Clearly:** Use "I" statements to express how you feel. For example, say, "I feel hurt when you cancel our plans at the last minute," instead of, "You never care about our plans."

- **Seek to Understand, Not to Win:** The goal of resolving a conflict is not to win but to understand and find a solution that works for both. Understanding will help you maintain the friendship.

- **Take Time to Cool Off If Need Be:** If emotions run high, it's okay to take a break and revisit the discussion later. This break can prevent saying things in the heat of the moment that you may regret.

- **Compromise:** When there's a disagreement, finding a middle ground that works for both sides is the key to sorting things out. By compromising, everyone feels heard and happy with the solution.

- **Forgive and Move Forward:** After sorting things out, let go of grudges. Holding onto past drama can poison future interactions. Move forward, not backward.

Conflict Resolution in Real-Time

Imagine this: It's Labor Day weekend. Your best friend, Hannah, heads off on a beach trip without shooting you an invite. You feel so hurt and angry with her that you give her the silent treatment for three whole weeks.

Even though she's blowing up your phone, trying to explain, you're not having it. You feel completely neglected, and you're left wondering why she didn't ask you to join her for the weekend. Calls and explanations from Hannah are met with silence from you—no matter how hard she tries.

Let's rewind and think about a different plot twist. If you'd spoken up about feeling left out and let Hannah explain herself—she genuinely thought you were away with your parents that weekend—the entire misunderstanding could have been avoided. Instead of moping around for three lonely weeks without your partner in crime, you could have been hanging out and having fun, steering clear of all that unnecessary drama.

What's the lesson here? Don't keep things bottled up inside. Always share your feelings when something is wrong, and work to sort out conflicts using techniques such as staying calm, being respectful, and expressing your feelings clearly.

Ending Toxic Friendships

Friendships are meant to enrich our lives, offer support, and bring joy. However, certain friendships can turn sour, becoming more draining than fulfilling. These are often referred to as *toxic friendships*. Understanding the difference between a healthy and a toxic friendship is imperative for your well-being.

A toxic friendship consistently leaves you feeling drained, criticized, or belittled. Unlike healthy friendships, where there's mutual respect and support, toxic friendships are often one-sided. They're characterized by negativity, lack of support, and emotional exhaustion.

Here are some signs that might indicate a friendship is toxic:

- **Constant Negativity:** If interactions with a friend leave you constantly unhappy or drained, it could be a red flag. You should only surround yourself with people who bring good vibes and laughter into your life.

- **Lack of Support:** Watch out for friends who are dismissive of your feelings or achievements. Someone who rolls their eyes when you share your excitement or even displays jealousy towards you could lead to an unhealthy relationship.

- **One-Sidedness:** If you find that you are always the one planning hangouts and reaching out first, a toxic relationship could develop. Remember, friendships should feel like a two-way street, not a solo mission.

- **Manipulative Behaviors:** Steer clear of people who often try to control or manipulate you; you deserve friends who respect your choices and don't play mind games.

- **Disrespect:** Consistent disrespect for your boundaries, feelings, or life choices are signs of an unhealthy relationship. Be aware of anyone who ignores your needs.

Toxic Friendships in Real-Time

Taylor and Morgan, the dynamic duo for years, find themselves at a crossroads as their rock-solid friendship takes an unexpected turn. Lately, Taylor's noticed a lot of negativity creeping into their hangouts, replacing the usual laughter with a weird vibe that leaves Taylor feeling drained.

Sharing exciting news doesn't bring the usual high-fives anymore. Instead, Morgan's response is dismissive, with an eye roll that hints at a lack of support. It's not the two-way street it used to be, and now Taylor's the one doing all the planning and reaching out.

To make things trickier, Taylor senses some manipulative vibes from Morgan. Morgan subtly exerts control, influencing Taylor's choices and playing mind games that tarnish the trust between them. Boundaries and feelings? It's like Morgan's forgotten they matter.

Recognizing the unmistakable signs of toxicity, Taylor faces the harsh truth that her once-close friend has become a source of drama and negativity. Knowing toxic friendships can mess with mental health,

Taylor decides it's time to close this chapter and focus on personal well-being.

If you recognize these signs in a friendship, it may be time to reconsider the relationship. Ending a toxic friendship can be challenging but necessary for your mental and emotional health. Here's a guide to approaching this situation:

- **Reflect on the Friendship:** Take some time to think about the friendship and why it feels toxic. Be honest with yourself about the impact on your well-being.

- **Communicate Your Feelings:** If you feel safe doing so, have an honest conversation with your friend. Express your feelings calmly and clearly. Use the "I" statements mentioned earlier in the chapter to explain how their actions make you feel.

- **Set Boundaries:** If you're not ready to completely end the friendship, try setting clear boundaries. Communicate these boundaries to your friend and stick to them.

- **Be Firm and Respectful:** If you decide to end the friendship, be firm but respectful in your decision. You can express gratitude for the good times while explaining that you need to move on for your well-being.

- **Seek Support:** Ending a friendship can be painful. Reach out to your crew of people for support. See Chapter 2 if you need a refresher on building a team of people who have your back.

- **Take Time for Yourself:** Allow yourself time to grieve the loss of the friendship. It's okay to feel sad or upset.

- **Focus on Positive Relationships:** Invest time and energy in healthy relationships that make you feel good about yourself.

- **Learn From the Experience:** Reflect on what you've learned from this friendship and how it can guide your future relationships.

Ending a toxic friendship is not a failure; it's a brave step towards taking care of your mental and emotional health. Everyone deserves friendships that are supportive, respectful, and uplifting. Letting go of unhealthy relationships opens space for healthier, more fulfilling connections in your life.

———

As we close this chapter on the complexities and joys of friendship, it's important to recognize that the skills we've discussed go far beyond just maintaining friendships. They are life skills valuable in every interaction and relationship you will encounter.

The lessons of listening, honesty, setting boundaries, and resolving conflicts are not just for navigating friendships. These skills build stronger family relationships, set the stage for romantic connections, and help you level up in the professional world.

As we move to the next chapter, we'll explore how these skills apply in other areas of life. From family dynamics to the class-room and casual hangouts, these skills are your tools for building a fulfilling and respectful life. They are the keys that will help you flourish in the vast world of human relationships.

CHAPTER 6
LEVERAGE SOCIAL SKILLS (L)

Welcome to Chapter 6, where you'll discover how to maximize your newly learned social skills. I'll guide you through applying the lessons you've been learning and get them to work for you in your day-to-day life. Whether navigating a crowded school hallway, chatting with new people at a party, or figuring out how to deal with family at home, this chapter will provide all the necessary tools.

We're going to talk about how to use your newfound skills to become adaptable in a variety of social situations, build resilience during setbacks, and navigate through misunderstandings. So, get ready to take your social game to the next level!

ADAPTABILITY: CHANGING WITH THE TIMES

What is Adaptability?

Adaptability is all about rolling with the punches and tweaking how you behave to match your environment. Being adaptable is super important because it helps us handle challenging situations and build great connections with people.

Being adaptable is not about changing who you are – it's more like adjusting your approach to match the scene. It's the skill that helps you read the room, get a feel for the mood and tone, and respond most fittingly.

Adaptability in Social Work

To properly illustrate adaptability, let's look at the role of a social worker. You may wonder why we're talking about social workers when this book is for teenagers. However, social workers are some of the most adaptable people out there.

On a typical day, they must deal with a wide range of people, from children to older adults, each with unique needs and backgrounds. A social worker's ability to adapt their approach to match each situation is essential.

For example, if they're helping out a kid in foster care, their approach must be nurturing and reassuring. But if it's a teen dealing with substance abuse, they might need to adapt their strategy to be more straight-up and factual.

Adaptability is a super power here—it not only helps in getting the message across but also in building trust, which is crucial in social work.

This skill isn't just for social work, though. It's a life skill. Being adaptable helps you handle all the twists and turns of human interactions, turning you into a super effective communicator and a seriously empathetic person.

And you know what? This skill gets better with practice. As you meet different people and face new situations, just keep in mind that adjusting is the way to go.

In summary, watch, learn, and be ready to tweak your approach depending on your environment.

. . .

Adaptability in Real-Time

Josh faced an unexpected challenge while visiting his grandfather's tranquil lakeside cabin. Accustomed to the hustle and bustle of loud hangouts with his friends, he realized the need for adaptability in this zen-like environment. So, when spending time with his grandfather, Josh toned down his usual excitement and enjoyed the quiet surrounding the cabin.

Engaging in hushed conversations, he found a different yet meaningful way to connect with his grandfather. Through adaptability, Josh learned to navigate the emotional nuances of the lakeside cabin, bringing solace to his grandfather and deepening their bond against the backdrop of nature's serenity.

As you can see from Josh's story, he adjusted his approach during his visit with his grandfather, changed his tone to calm and serene, and tweaked his behavior to match the mood. When we adapt to different environments, we strengthen our connections and foster meaningful moments.

In the following sections, we're going to dive into other key aspects of social skills, such as building resilience and handling difficult social situations, further enhancing your ability to succeed in the social world.

Reading the Room

Reading the room is another form of adaptability. It involves tuning into the mood of a social situation and catching the unspoken signals. Observe how people are standing or sitting, listen to how they talk, and get a feel for the overall vibe. Is everyone relaxed and cracking jokes, or is the tone more serious? Changing how you act to match the room's mood can improve your social game.

Let's take a look at a scenario where reading the room worked out beautifully for you.

Reading the Room: Triumph in Action

So, there you were, stepping into the lively school cafeteria, ready to join a table of new friends for lunch. The room was buzzing with energy — some students were deep into conversation, while others focused on their phones or homework.

As you took a moment to read the room, you noticed a mix of relaxed vibes and bursts of laughter. Everyone seemed laid-back and approachable, so you decided to match the mood. With a grin, you greeted your new friends with an easygoing "Hey, what's up?"

As you joined the conversation, you effortlessly picked up on the friendly banter and casual tone. You threw in a few jokes and shared some light-hearted stories, keeping the atmosphere fun and upbeat. The room's mood became infectious, and soon, everyone was laughing and enjoying the moment.

Your ability to read the room and adapt to the laid back vibes made you feel right at home. Tuning into the unspoken signals, you not only connected with your peers but also showed that you could roll with the social flow, making lunchtime a memorable and enjoyable experience for everyone around you.

Now let's take a look at the same scenario, but this time, you fail to pick up on the subtle cues of the lunch room.

Reading the Room: An Epic Fail

So, there you were, walking into that same lively school cafeteria, excited to join a table of new friends for lunch.

But, unfortunately, this time, you completely misread the room. Despite the casual and relaxed atmosphere, you charged in with an over-enthusiastic "Yo, what's up, party people?" The response was a few awkward glances and forced smiles.

As you joined the conversation, you failed to pick up on the subtle cues. Your attempts at humor fell flat, and your light-hearted stories seemed out of sync with the prevailing mood. The room's atmosphere became noticeably awkward, and the once-lively chatter dwindled into uncomfortable silence.

Your inability to read the room left you feeling out of place. The unspoken signals were lost on you, and your efforts to match the vibes of the room ended up making lunchtime a cringe-worthy experience for everyone involved.

What's the takeaway here? Being attuned to subtle nuances can be critical in making or breaking a social situation, as illustrated by the two different outcomes in the cafeteria scenario.

But don't worry, in the next section, we'll look at how building resilience can help us bounce back from any social blunder because, let's face it, no matter how excellent your social skills are, we all face social challenges from time to time.

BUILDING RESILIENCE: BOUNCING BACK FROM SOCIAL SETBACKS

Resilience in social interactions requires bouncing back from tough times, handling pressure, and adapting to difficult situations. Besides getting through complex challenges, you will learn from these experiences and grow. In the next section, we're going to explore how to build up resilience, a skill that will change the way you handle your social life.

Understanding Resilience in Social Contexts

We often think of resilience in terms of big life challenges, but it's incredibly important in day-to-day social interactions. When you are resilient, you can deal with a friend's hurtful words, manage rejection, and shake off a social blunder. Resilient people can take challenges in stride and become stronger in the end.

Let's take a look at how resilience looks in real life.

Building Resilience in Real-Time

As a teenager trying to figure out the complex world of high school, I used to overthink every single conversation and interaction. It was like being a detective, obsessively analyzing every word and action. Like a broken record, I would replay conversations over and over in my head.

In my mind, I'd blow up these tiny social slip-ups into something much bigger. This habit of dwelling on every little thing really messed with how I acted in the moment and approached new situations.

Eventually, I learned that obsessing over these so-called setbacks worsened things. The scenarios I made up in my head were way off from reality. Learning to be resilient meant understanding that these bumps in the road happen, but they don't have to be the end of the world.

I started to see these little social mess-ups not as disasters but as chances to learn and grow. I learned to move on and not let these issues control my social life. I adopted a motto that I still use today: "Move forward, not backward." Forgive yourself for your social blunders, learn from them, and move on.

So, bouncing back from those awkward social moments might seem like a breeze in theory, but you might be wondering, *"How on earth do I actually pull it off?"* Well, worry not. Let's check out some simple tricks to help you become more resilient in handling those social hiccups.

· · ·

Strategies for Building Social Resilience

- **Learning From Past Mistakes:** Reflect on past social setbacks. Instead of asking yourself, "Why am I such an idiot?" ask yourself, "What can I learn from this? "Learning from these experiences can help you handle future situations effectively.

- **Practicing Self-Compassion:** Be kind to yourself. Understand that everyone faces social challenges, and it's okay to make mistakes.

- **Focusing on What You Can Control:** In any difficult social situation, focus on your actions and reactions, not changing someone else's.

- **Cultivating a Positive Outlook:** Try to find the silver lining in challenging situations. A positive mindset can help you navigate through and recover from social setbacks.

- **Reach Out to Your Support Network:** In Chapter 2, you learned about setting up a solid support network of friends and family who will have your back no matter what. Now's the time to reach out to this network of people who will provide encouragement, perspective, and strength during tough times. They will be your anchor and help you to become your most resilient self.

Let's take a look at some common social setbacks and how you can apply these resilience strategies in your life.

How You Can Apply Social Resilience in Your Life

- **Facing Rejection:** Picture not making the cut for a school club you were excited about (ouch!). Instead of getting stuck in the disappointment, turn it into an opportunity to explore other interests and meet new people. Use the experience to strengthen your resilience, knowing that setbacks can lead to exciting new paths and unexpected friendships.

- **Friendship Drama:** Recall the beach trip drama from earlier? Now, envision a resilient response. Instead of feeling down about your friends' beach outing without you, imagine bouncing back, shaking off the FOMO, and reaching out to your friend to mend things. Resilience means swiftly addressing conflicts, allowing you to move on and enjoy time with your friends without dwelling on the past.

- **Your Response to Criticism:** You just received criticism from a group project member, and you initially feel defensive. But after considering the feedback, you recognize areas where you could improve, leading to better collaboration in the group.

Building resilience is a journey of self-discovery and growth. It's about developing the inner strength to face social challenges head-on, learning from them, and emerging stronger and wiser. As we cultivate resilience, we equip ourselves with a powerful tool that enhances our social interactions and enriches our relationships.

DEALING WITH DIFFICULT SOCIAL SITUATIONS

Social interactions are not always smooth sailing. Sometimes, they can be challenging, filled with awkward silences, misunderstandings, or even confrontations — don't worry, I've got you. In the following pages, I'll show you how to navigate these situations with grace and tact.

Awkward Silences

Awkward silences can be daunting, but they're a common part of human interaction. Embracing these quiet moments can actually foster deeper connections and understanding between people. It's during these pauses that people often have the opportunity to reflect on the conversation, allowing for more thoughtful responses and a genuine exchange of ideas.

Rather than viewing them as uncomfortable, consider awkward silences as natural breaks that give both people the chance to absorb information and contribute meaningfully to the ongoing dialogue. By navigating these moments with patience and openness, you can create a more authentic and enriching communication experience.

Handling Awkward Silences

- **Embrace the Silence:** Having moments of silence in a conversation is okay. It doesn't always mean something is wrong.

- **Change the Topic:** If a particular topic isn't sparking interest, shift to something else. Ask about a favorite hobby or recent movie they've seen.

- **Ask Open-Ended Questions:** These questions encourage detailed responses and can revive a dying conversation.

- **Use Humor:** A light, well-placed joke can ease the tension and bring a smile to everyone (just remember to read the room first).

Navigating Misunderstandings

Misunderstandings can sometimes spiral into unnecessary conflicts fueled by miscommunication and assumptions. In a world filled with fast-paced conversations and quick texts, it's easy for messages to get mixed up, leading to confusion. These misinterpretations can create tension and hurt feelings, especially when emotions run high. Let's take a look at a misunderstanding in real-time.

Misunderstandings in Real-Time

Ben: Hey, Mike! Haven't seen you around lately. What's going on?

Mike: Hey, yeah, been kinda busy. Oh, by the way, thanks for inviting me to the party last weekend.

Ben: Party? What party?

Mike: The one at your place. You know, Saturday night?

Ben: Dude, I didn't have a party on Saturday. Are you sure it was my place?

Mike: Uh, yeah. I got a text from you saying to come over for a laid-back get-together.

Ben: That's so weird. I didn't send any invites. Maybe someone else organized something?

Mike: Well, when I got there, your sister said you were busy but told me to join in. It was awkward; I thought you were mad at me or something.

Ben: Wait, my sister? Oh, I think I know what happened. She must've organized some sort of hangout without telling me. I had no clue.

Mike: Seriously? I felt so out of place, and then I thought you didn't want me there.

Ben: Mike, I had no idea about it. My sister probably thought she was doing me a favor. I'm really sorry you felt that way.

Mike: It's cool. I just thought... you know, maybe I messed up or something.

Ben: Nah, man. It's a misunderstanding. Let's hang out this weekend, just us. I'll make up for it.

Mike: Sounds good. Thanks for clearing that up, though. I was stressing about it.

Ben: No worries, dude. We're good.

Notice how this misunderstanding was cleared up maturely and respectfully. Remember the following tips when clearing up misunderstandings with friends.

Tips for Clearing Up Misunderstandings:

- **Listen First:** Understand the other person's perspective before jumping to conclusions.

- **Clarify Your Point:** If you feel misunderstood, calmly explain your point of view.

- **Apologize if Necessary:** A simple apology can often resolve a misunderstanding and show that you value the relationship.

- **Agree to Disagree:** Not all misunderstandings will be resolved. Sometimes, it's best to respectfully agree to disagree.

Knowing When to Walk Away

Sometimes, the best option is to remove yourself from a difficult situation:

- **If It's Unproductive:** If the conversation is going nowhere, it might be time to step away.

- **If It's Unhealthy:** If the interaction harms your mental or emotional well-being, walking away is a valid choice.

- **Give Time to Cool Off:** Sometimes, a break can give both parties time to calm down and think more clearly.

Dealing with difficult social situations is a part of life. By approaching these challenges with understanding, patience, and a willingness to find common ground, you can navigate the trickiest interactions successfully. Every challenge is an opportunity to learn and develop your social skills.

———

As we close this chapter on navigating the complexities of social interactions, we embrace a new horizon. You've now equipped yourself with invaluable life skills: adaptability in changing circumstances, resilience in the face of setbacks, and the art of handling misunderstandings.

These skills are more than just tools for social success; they are the keys to unlocking a life filled with richer experiences and deeper connections.

Looking ahead, Chapter 7 opens the door to applying these skills in ways that can enrich your life. You will take these concepts beyond mere theory and bring them into the everyday tapestry of your life. This next chapter is about turning your learned skills into habits that shape a life you love.

Imagine a life where challenges become opportunities for growth, where every interaction is a chance to learn and improve, and where your relationships are sources of joy and support — this is the life that awaits you.

So, let's turn the page together and explore how these social skills can build a life that is not only successful but also fulfilling and joyous. Get ready to embark on a journey where each day is an opportunity to apply what you've learned and make a meaningful difference in your life and the lives of those around you.

CHAPTER 7
LIVE A LIFE YOU WANT

> "The greatest thing in the world is to know how to belong to oneself." – Michel de Montaigne

This insightful quote encapsulates the essence of our final chapter's theme: finding authentic happiness and fulfillment, whether in the company of others or in the solace of one's own company.

SOCIAL WELL-BEING: A CONTINUOUS JOURNEY

Social well-being is a journey, not a destination. It's a continuous process that evolves as you grow and change. It's not about reaching a point where you're suddenly 'socially well' and then stopping; it's about constant effort and time dedicated to nurturing your social health.

So, what does a healthy social life entail? It begins with finding meaningful connections rather than popularity. You must find friends who support, challenge, and help you grow.

A healthy social life requires a balance between socializing and solitude. Being able to reflect and be happy in your own time is just as important as finding connections. This balance is crucial because it prevents dependency on others for your well-being.

FINDING HAPPINESS AND FULFILLMENT

The pursuit of happiness and fulfillment is a universal quest, and social success plays a significant role in it. But let's be clear: social success isn't just about how many friends you have; it's finding genuine joy and fulfillment in your interactions and relationships.

True happiness centers on being connected, understood, and valued when in the presence of others. It's about enjoying shared laughter over an inside joke, the comfort of a familiar face in the crowd, or the warmth from a heartfelt conversation. These moments, big or small, enrich our lives and add layers to our happiness.

· · ·

Here are some tips to find joy in your social life:

- **Value Quality Over Quantity:** Focus on deepening meaningful relationships rather than increasing your friend count. A few close friends can provide more happiness than dozens of acquaintances.

- **Be Yourself:** Authenticity attracts others to you. When you are true to yourself, you attract people who appreciate the real you, leading to fulfilling interactions.

- **Active Participation:** Be an active participant in your social interactions. Ask questions, show interest, and share your thoughts. Getting involved in the discussions makes socializing more enjoyable and meaningful.

- **Find Shared Interests:** Bond over common hobbies or interests. Whether it's a sport, a book club, or a cooking class, shared activities create enjoyable experiences and strengthen connections.

- **Practice Empathy:** Show genuine interest in others' lives. Understanding and empathizing with their experiences can deepen bonds and enhance your own social satisfaction.

- **Positive Mindset:** Approach social interactions with a positive attitude. A positive outlook can make socializing more enjoyable and attract positivity from others.

Fulfilling social interactions plays a massive role in overall life satisfaction. Deep and meaningful friendships provide support, broaden our perspectives, and contribute to our sense of belonging. Sharing experiences with others teaches us about compassion, understanding, and the joy of spending time together.

STRIKING A BALANCE: SOCIAL LIFE AND SCHOOL LIFE

Creating a fulfilling life is like walking a tightrope — balance is essential. For teenagers, this balance often revolves around juggling time spent with friends, school work, extracurricular activities or jobs, and family priorities. And the digital world throws in distractions like social media and binge-watching shows.

So, what's the trick to keeping all these balls in the air? The secret is *time management*. Once you have time management under control, you can allocate time and energy to your social circle and other things like schoolwork without letting one overshadow the other. You *can* have your cake and eat it, too.

Achieving this balance might seem challenging, but it is doable with the right strategies. Let's look at some techniques to balance your social life.

Time Management Strategy #1: The Pomodoro Technique

Time management is the cornerstone of balance. The *Pomodoro Technique* is your secret time management weapon, perfect for balancing school, social life, and personal time. Imagine breaking your day into short, focused sprints, maximizing your energy and attention.

Named after the Italian word for tomato, the Pomodoro Technique derives its name from the tomato-shaped kitchen timer used by its creator, Francesco Cirillo. This technique involves breaking your day into short, focused sprints to enhance productivity and energy.

Here's what to do:

1. Grab a timer – maybe your phone – and set it for 25 minutes, also known as a *Pomodoro*. You're all in during this time, giving 100% to a single task, like conquering that math assignment or diving into a reading session.

2. Once the timer dings, take a short break, about 5 minutes. It's your chance to recharge, scroll through memes, or have a nice stretch.

3. After completing four Pomodoros, treat yourself to a more extended break, around 15-30 minutes. You've earned it. The trick is to focus intensely during those 25-minute bursts, knowing a break is just around the corner.

This technique keeps you motivated, prevents burnout, and turns your to-do list into a game. Plus, it's flexible. Adjust the times based on your preferences and needs. The Pomodoro Technique transforms your study sessions, helping you tackle tasks efficiently and leaving plenty of time for the things you love.

Pomodoro Technique in Real-Time

Tackling an Algebra Assignment

1. **Start of the Study Session:**

- Set the timer for 25 minutes (Pomodoro).
- Begin working on solving algebraic equations and completing the assigned problems.

2. **During the Pomodoro (25 minutes):**

- Dive deep into the algebra assignment, solving equations and working through the problems.
- Stay focused and avoid checking your phone or getting distracted.

3. **End of the Pomodoro (Timer Dings):**

- When the timer goes off, take a 5-minute break.
- Stand up, stretch, grab a snack, or do a quick relaxation exercise to recharge.

4. **Second Pomodoro:**

- Set the timer for another 25 minutes.
- Continue with the algebra assignment, perhaps moving on to more complex problems or reviewing challenging concepts.

5. End of the Second Pomodoro (Timer Dings)

- Take another 5-minute break.
- Use this time to refresh your mind, maybe do a quick walk around the room, and check your messages.

6. Third and Fourth Pomodoros:

- Repeat the process for the third and fourth Pomodoros, each followed by a 5-minute break.
- Stay engaged with the algebra assignment, progressing in a structured and focused manner.

7. After Four Pomodoros:

- Take a more extended break of 15-30 minutes.
- During this break, reward yourself with a snack, a short workout, or do something enjoyable to relax your mind.

8. Flexibility:

- Adjust the duration of the Pomodoros and breaks based on your personal preferences and energy levels. Feel free to experiment with different time intervals if you find 25 minutes too short or too long. The key is to find a rhythm that maximizes your productivity and prevents burnout.

Time Management Strategy #2: Get Organized

Another powerful way to strike a balance in your life is by getting organized. Begin by crafting a schedule, prioritizing tasks, and methodically breaking down your goals. Soon enough, you'll master setting priorities—a valuable skill for a lifetime. The key is finding a schedule that works for you, empowering you to control your time. Now, let's explore the steps to enhance your organizational skills.

1. Get a Planner or Use a Digital Calendar: Start by getting a physical planner or using a digital calendar app on your phone or computer. Choose whatever feels more comfortable for you. This will be your go-to tool for organizing your schedule.

2. List All Tasks: Write down all your tasks, including school assignments, extracurricular activities, chores, and any other responsibilities you have. Make sure to include fun activities or downtime, too. This gives you a clear picture of everything you need to manage.

3. Categorize Tasks: Divide your tasks into school, hobbies, chores, and personal time. This helps you see where your time is going and ensures you don't overlook anything important.

4. Set Realistic Goals: For each task, set realistic and achievable goals. Break down bigger tasks into smaller, manageable steps. This makes your goals more achievable and helps you avoid feeling overwhelmed.

5. Assign Time Blocks: Allocate specific time blocks for different activities. For example, if you have homework, schedule an exact time to focus on it. Be realistic about the time each task might take, and don't forget to include breaks.

6. Prioritize Tasks: Now comes the crucial part—prioritize your tasks. Identify the most important and time-sensitive ones. These are your top priorities. List them at the top of your schedule or give them specific time slots.

7. Regularly Review and Adjust: Your schedule isn't set in stone. Periodically review your priorities and schedule to make sure everything is on track. Life can be unpredictable, so be ready to adjust your schedule as needed.

. . .

8. Use Alerts and Reminders: If you're using a digital calendar, set up alerts and reminders. This ensures you complete important deadlines and remember tasks. It's like having a personal assistant to keep you on track.

9. Learn to Say No: Part of setting priorities is knowing when to say no. If your schedule is getting too packed and affecting your ability to focus or enjoy personal time, declining additional commitments is okay.

10. Reflect and Adjust: At the end of each week, take some time to evaluate how well you stuck to your schedule and if any adjustments are needed. Reflect on what worked and didn't, and use this insight to improve your scheduling skills.

When thinking about your schedule, don't burn yourself out. Your schedule should never be about squeezing in time for *study study study*. It's about being honest with yourself. Make a schedule with time for hitting the books *and* kicking back with friends or relaxing. You are in the driver's seat to create a schedule that is the perfect balance for you.

Achieving balance means finding harmony in various parts of your life. It's all about relishing the adventure of growing, acquiring new knowledge, forming friendships, and uncovering your true self. Keep in mind that balance isn't a static condition; instead, it's an ongoing adventure of adapting and aligning. When you master balancing, you pave the way for a satisfying and enriched life.

EMBRACING YOUR JOURNEY

The path to a fulfilling life is not a straight line; it's a mosaic of experiences, each piece significant. In this chapter, you've delved into what it means to find true happiness in friendships and the importance of balance between your social and personal life.

As we prepare to tie all these pieces together, it's essential to carry forward the lessons learned, the skills honed, and the insights gained. These tools will help you navigate the complexities of life, build meaningful relationships, and find your own sense of happiness and fulfillment.

THE EASY WAY TO HELP SOMEONE WHO IS STRUGGLING

Teens yearn for a lively group of friends, people with whom to connect, and the confidence to build bonds based on shared interests, laughter, and trust. Let those who are battling social anxiety know that overcoming it involves harnessing a select set of strategies that produce real results.

Simply by sharing your honest opinion of this book and a little about your own experiences, you'll show new readers that they're not alone – and you'll point them in the direction of the resource they need to transform their social lives.

Thank you so much for your support. It has more of an impact than you realize.

>>> Scan the QR code below to leave your review on Amazon.

CONCLUSION

I hope you've found valuable insights and inspiration and that you're walking away with a new-found, unshakable confidence. Above all, I hope you'll embrace yourself from now on—all of you —because the world is such a better place with your uniqueness.

As we draw this book to a close, it's time to reflect on the transformative path we've traveled together through *The Social Teen*. This book was never just about learning social skills; it was about embarking on a profound exploration of personal growth and social mastery.

The SOCIAL framework, intricately woven into every chapter, was designed not as a mere set of instructions but as a compass guiding you toward a richer, more connected life.

We began this adventure understanding the deep-seated challenges of shyness and social anxiety that many teenagers face. Step by step, through self-awareness, overcoming obstacles, crafting conversations, initiating interactions, assembling authentic friendships, and leveraging life skills, we've seen a transformation unfold. It's a shift from the shadows of hesitation to the sunlight of confidence, from the sidelines of social gatherings to the heart of meaningful connections.

This book aimed to light a path from the uncertainty and isolation often felt during teenage years to a place of confidence and belonging. As you turn the last page, remember that your progress doesn't end here. The SOCIAL framework is more than a method; it's a gateway to a life rich in relationships and self-assuredness, where each interaction is an opportunity, and every moment is a step towards becoming the socially adept individual you aspire to be.

In our exploration of the SOCIAL framework, we delved into each facet, unraveling its significance and impact on your path to finding social confidence and competence.

Here is a quick summary of everything in the SOCIAL framework:

Start With Self-Awareness: Self-awareness lays the groundwork for all social skills. Recognizing your emotions, strengths, and areas for growth enables you to navigate social landscapes with clarity and purpose. Understanding yourself sets the stage for understanding others, paving the way for genuine connections.

Overcome Obstacles: Overcoming obstacles is about resilience through facing fears and challenging social anxiety, emerging stronger in the end. This step is crucial in transforming perceived barriers into stepping stones, helping you to move beyond your comfort zone into a realm of growth and confidence.

Craft Confident Conversations: Mastering the art of conversation is key to unlocking social doors. Conversation goes beyond just talking; it's about listening, engaging, and connecting. Through this step, you learn the dance of dialogue, where exchanging words becomes a bridge to understanding and rapport.

Initiate Interactions: The courage to initiate interactions is a social game-changer. You are taking the lead in your social life, stepping forward to make the first move, and embracing the opportunities that come with new connections.

Assemble Authentic Friendships: Building and maintaining genuine friendships is the heart of your social life. Friendships form through mutual respect, shared interests, and sincere care. These friendships are the pillars of your social network, offering support, joy, and a sense of belonging.

Leverage Life Skills: Finally, leveraging life skills is about applying what you've learned in various aspects of your life. You adapt your newfound social prowess to different contexts, whether in school, at home, or in future workplaces, ensuring you can thrive in any social setting.

Each step of the SOCIAL method is a building block in the architecture of your social development. Together, these blocks form a comprehensive toolkit that empowers you to navigate the complexities of teenage social life with confidence and grace.

Now, it's your turn to take the reins. You've navigated through The Social Teen's pages, absorbing the principles of the SOCIAL method. But remember, true transformation begins with action. Start small, applying these lessons in your everyday life. Challenge yourself to initiate a conversation, join a new group, or practice active listening in your next interaction. Each small step is a leap towards building your confidence and honing your social skills.

As you reflect on the insights and strategies shared in *The Social Teen*, I invite you to share your thoughts and experiences. Your feedback is invaluable to me as an author and others embarking on their social journeys. By leaving a review, you contribute to a larger conversation, helping guide and inspire peers who may be navigating similar challenges. Your perspective can make a meaningful difference, offering encouragement and insight to those seeking to transform their social lives. I sincerely appreciate your time and thoughts in sharing a review. Thank you for being a part of this journey.

As we conclude this book together, remember: your social journey is uniquely yours, but you don't walk it alone. Every step you take with the courage to connect, grow, and be authentically you, lights the path for others to follow. So go forth with the confidence that you have everything within you to create the fulfilling social life you envision. In the words of Helen Keller, "*Alone we can do so little; together we can do so much.*" Embrace your path, embrace each other, and watch the world open before you.

REFERENCES

Ackerman, C. E. (2020, April 1). What Is Self-Awareness? (+5 Ways to Be More Self-Aware). Positive Psychology. https://positivepsychology.com/self-awareness-matters-how-you-can-be-more-self-aware/

Adelmann, M., & Berger, C. R. (2014). Adventures in Social Research: Data Analysis Using IBM SPSS Statistics. Sage Publications.

Anwar, Y. (2020, December 16). The 16 Facial Expressions Most Common to Emotional Situations Worldwide. Berkeley News. https://news.berkeley.edu/2020/12/16/the-16-facial-expressions-most-common-to-emotional-situations-worldwide

Arzt, N. (2023, January 26). Shyness Vs. Social Anxiety: Understanding the Difference. Choosing Therapy. https://www.choosingtherapy.com/social-anxiety-vs-shyness/

Barker, E. (2016). Barking Up the Wrong Tree: The Surprising Science Behind Why Everything You Know About Success Is (Mostly) Wrong. HarperOne.

Barth, F. D. (2018, February 10). What Makes It so Hard to Walk Away From a Bad Situation? The Couch, Psychology Today. https://www.psychologytoday.com/us/blog/the-couch/201802/what-makes-it-so-hard-walk-away-bad-situation

Blankson, A. (2020, June 23). Are You Digitally Self-Aware? Psychology Today. https://www.psychologytoday.com/intl/blog/the-future-happiness/202006/are-you-digitally-self-aware

Boothman, N. (2014). Convince Them in 90 Seconds or Less: Make Instant Connections That Pay Off in Business and in Life. Workman Publishing.

Campbell, L. (2023, April 26). Why Personal Boundaries are Important and How to Set Them. Psych Central. https://psychcentral.com/relationships/what-are-personal-boundaries-how-do-i-get-some

Carlucci, K. M. (2024, April 7). The Art of Adaptability – The Social Worker's Superpower. SocialWorker. https://www.socialworker.com/feature-articles/practice/adaptability-social-worker-superpower/

Carnegie, D. (2016). How to Win Friends and Influence People in the Digital Age. Simon & Schuster.

Casabianca, S. S. (2022, October 28). 7 Signs Someone Doesn't Respect Your Boundaries and What to Do. Psych Central. https://psychcentral.com/relationships/signs-boundary-violations#

Cherry, K. (2023, February 22). Types of Nonverbal Communication. Verywell Mind. https://www.verywellmind.com/types-of-nonverbal-communication-2795397

Connolly, B. (2016, March 18). The Most Interesting Conversations Have These 3

REFERENCES

Elements in Common. TIME. https://time.com/4259998/interesting-conversation-tips/

Danise, A. (2020, July 17). 13 Times In-Person Communication Is Better Than Electronic Exchanges. Forbes Coachescouncil. https://www.forbes.com/sites/forbescoachescouncil/2020/07/17/13-times-in-person-communication-is-better-than-electronic-exchanges/?sh=4825ca6f2eb7

David, M. (2023, September 29). The Confident Teen: A Practical Guide to Boost Your Confidence, Transform Your Self-Worth, and Take Control of Your Life. Marnie David.

Deupree, S. (2023, January 30). CBT for Social Anxiety: How It Works, Examples & Effectiveness. Choosing Therapy. https://www.choosingtherapy.com/cbt-for-social-anxiety/

Eurich, T. (2018, January 04). What Self-Awareness Really Is (and How to Cultivate It). Harvard Business Review. https://hbr.org/2018/01/what-self-awareness-really-is-and-how-to-cultivate-it

Field, B. (2023, July 13). How to Set Boundaries With Friends—and Why It's Necessary. Verywell Mind. https://www.verywellmind.com/how-to-set-boundaries-with-friends-7503205

Fleming, P., & Lampi, J. P. (2018). The Art of Conversation: Change Your Life with Confident Communication. Capstone.

Fine, D. (2015). The Fine Art of Small Talk: How to Start a Conversation, Keep It Going, Build Networking Skills - and Leave a Positive Impression!. Hachette Books.

Forsyth, J. P., & Eifert, G. H. (2016). The Mindfulness & Acceptance Workbook for Anxiety: A Guide to Breaking Free from Anxiety, Phobias, and Worry Using Acceptance

Goulston, M. (2015). Just Listen: Discover the Secret to Getting Through to Absolutely Anyone. AMACOM.

Greenberg, M. (2019, December 31). Does Being More Social Make Us Happier? The Mindful Self-Express. https://www.psychologytoday.com/intl/blog/the-mindful-self-express/201912/does-being-more-social-make-us-happier

Grieco, M. (2022, January 4). BALANCING SCHOOL AND SOCIAL LIFE. Simple Studies. https://www.simplestudies.org/blog/balancing-school-and-social-life

Hartney, E. (2023, June 28). 10 Basic Netiquette Rules. Verywell Mind. https://www.verywellmind.com/ten-rules-of-netiquette-22285

Headlee, C. (2017). We Need to Talk: How to Have Conversations That Matter. Harper Wave.

Hurley, K. (2022, October 21). Teenage Cell Phone Addiction: Are You Worried About Your Child? Psycom. https://www.psycom.net/cell-phone-internet-addiction

Karrass, C. L. (2013). The Negotiating Game: How to Get What You Want. Thomas Y. Crowell Company.

Kirmayer, M. (2022, May 23). 6 (Non-Awkward) Ways To Approach Someone You

REFERENCES

Want To Be Friends With. The Everygirl. https://theeverygirl.com/6-ways-to-approach-someone-you-want-to-be-friends-with/

Kraft, R. N. (2022, March 17). What Makes a Good Conversation? Contributed by: Robert N. Kraft Ph.D. Psychology Today. https://www.psychologytoday.com/us/blog/defining-memories/202203/what-makes-good-conversation

Kristenson, S. (2023, March 31). 25 Qualities of a Good Friend You Should Look For. Happier Human. https://www.happierhuman.com/qualities-good-friend/

Lawler, M. (2023, July 21). Why Friendships Are So Important for Health and Well-Being. Everyday Health. https://www.everydayhealth.com/emotional-health/social-support.aspx

Marie, S. (2022, August 26). 9 Ways to Solve Misunderstandings In a Relationship. PsychCentral. https://psychcentral.com/relationships/pointers-for-couples-to-prevent-resolve-misunderstandings

Mayo Clinic Staff. (2022, January 12). Friendships: Enrich your life and improve your health. Mayo Clinic. https://www.mayoclinic.org/healthy-lifestyle/adult-health/in-depth/friendships/art-20044860

Mayo Clinic Staff. (2022, July 14). Resilience: Build skills to endure hardship. Mayo Clinic. https://www.mayoclinic.org/tests-procedures/resilience-training/in-depth/resilience/art-20046311

McKay, B., & McKay, K. (2021, June 6). Social Briefing #8: How to Ask Open vs. Closed Questions. The Art of Manliness. https://www.artofmanliness.com/people/social-skills/social-briefing-8-better-conversations-asking-open-ended-questions/

Morningstar, A. (2023, October 26). 25 Qualities Of A Good Friend (That Show You Can Depend On Them). A Conscious Rethink. https://www.aconsciousrethink.com/7171/qualities-good-friend/

Nolan, M. B. (2022, June 28). The Art of Friendship: How to Address and Respond to Conflict. Shondaland. https://www.shondaland.com/live/family/a40436785/art-of-friendship-how-to-handle-conflict/

Pal, P., Hauck, C., Goldstein, E., Bobinet, K., & Bradley, C. (2018, August 27). 5 Simple Mindfulness Practices for Daily Life. Mindful. https://www.mindful.org/take-a-mindful-moment-5-simple-practices-for-daily-life/

Robert, R. (2023, May 26). Time Management for Teenagers. Time Hack Hero. https://timehackhero.com/time-management-for-teenagers/

www.ingramcontent.com/pod-product-compliance
Lightning Source LLC
Chambersburg PA
CBHW062119020426
42335CB00013B/1027

* 9 7 8 1 9 6 2 6 9 2 0 8 3 *